LIMIT BREAKER

101 Short Stories, Essays, and Insights
to Improve Communication Skills

ARMANITALKS 🎙️🔥

Table of Contents

Author's Preface

-To learn more about the universe, learn about the mind.
-To learn more about the mind, learn about the universe.

There's something deep about curiosity that does not register at first. I believe that we are sleeping on how powerful curiosity really is.

I came to realize in my early 20s that I could control my mindset, simply by smiling. When I would do a gentle smile, that's when I came to calm myself down. When discovering this little insight, I thought I entered a new portal.

For future high-pressure events, I would smile away.
Right before getting called on stage to give a speech, hold the smile. Right before I was about to enter a high stakes meeting at work, hold the smile. Right before I was going to conquer a fear, hold the smile.

It became evident to me that this tiny facial gesture was a superpower. However, very few talked about it.

I came to realize that all superpowers can have its critics as well.

There came a day when I was a part of a team meeting for a club. One of the senior leaders had a strange idea to build team harmony.

This club had a lot of internal conflict as of late. So, this team leader decided to create the **Hell Chamber.**

Within this Hell Chamber, each individual member would go up in front of all the other members. Then each of the other members would tell that member about their flaws.

So, let's say Johnny went centerstage.

The different members of the audience would be like:
-Johnny, you don't have the best attitude.
-You didn't attend the last 5 meetings on time.
-Johnny, you can be more present when you are here.

A part of you may be wondering what the point of this Hell Chamber was? Beats me! The guy who thought of it was clearly doing some experimenting.

By the time I got called on stage, I was nervous. This was a high-pressure meeting.

But I had my superpower, you know?
The smile.

As the members began criticizing my moves, I did what I knew best.
I smiled.

Most people let it slide. However, my facial gesture caught the eyes of a member named Vinnie.

By the time it was Vinnie's time to share his thoughts about me, he said:
'Everyone. Just look at Armani's face. He has been doing this pompous smirk this entire time. He just can't ever take anything seriously.'

Being the followers that they were, the other members agreed like sheep.

I finally found a hole in this superpower.
Sometimes, a smile could be perceived as making light of a situation.

This hole was not enough to make me stop. As a matter of fact, this flaw simply made me build **more** faith regarding this beautiful move.

Who cares if I made light of the high-pressure situation? That's what allows me to thrive, Vinnie, you silly rabbit.

"Curiosity killed the cat."
That's been the negative stigma regarding curiosity.

"You shouldn't be too curious now; it can get you in trouble," they say.
Is this true?

Sure.
I guess being too curious can get you in predicaments that you shouldn't have been in.

However, as discussed earlier... even superpowers have its flaws. Just gotta' decided which flaws are worth it.

Curiosity has always been worth it. It's the magical force that turns a closed mind into an unlimited mind. It is the force which turns someone who is losing a zest for life into a born-again warrior.

Most importantly, it's the force out there that can turn a person who hasn't escaped the comfort zone into a Limit Breaker.

The Nature of the Mind

I came to realize that curiosity is not an option.
It is something that is engrained within humans.

Throughout my life, I've seen many transitions of people take place. I'm sure you have too.

What's some of the spooky transitions among people that you know? What are some of the somber transitions?

For me, 2 stick out:
-People who I wouldn't have expected committing heinous crimes, committing heinous crimes.
-Death.

That's one of the dark parts of growing up. You see some people fade away either spiritually or physically. By the way, don't worry, I'm going to share the light shortly.

I've heard about 2 very shocking crimes from people who I used to know.

They weren't good friends or anything. I still knew them though. Enough to be like, *'Yo, I went to school with that kid,'* when this particular atrocious crime was announced.

The 2 shocking crimes ranged from kidnapping to murder.

Those moments allowed me to see that people can change, but not always for the best.

Another unfortunate truth is regarding death.
Close ones who died unexpectedly.
Maybe from a car accident, killed or a sickness.
These are the dark transitions.

A shade below this degree of darkness is gossiping.

You ever met someone like that? All they could do like an all-star was gossip.

At this point of your life, you've changed. You've read books, invested in a purpose, and started taking your fitness seriously.

However, a close friend, or maybe even a spouse, has not changed their ways. They transitioned for the worst. Constantly talking about other people and trying to drag you into it.

People don't only grow apart due to distance.
It's also due to mental content.

These 2 people who were once close just ran out of things to talk about.

I'm not over here making fun of people who gossip incessantly. Whenever I see multiple people from different parts of the world doing a similar behavior, I use this as a compass to learn about the human psyche.

Why are so many people gossiping?
What is gossiping....?

I have an answer.
- Gossiping = Curiosity + Gravity.

Don't you see?

The mind was programmed towards curiosity. You get to decide which direction to point that curiosity towards. When a direction is not assigned, the mind gets pulled down by gravity.

In this scenario, gravity represents:
- Limited beliefs.
- Gossip.
- Drama.
- And all that other hoopla that the masses are entrenched in.

Curiosity was never a choice. In one way shape or form, the mental faculties will be pulled in a direction. That's just the nature of the mind.

Most people live life this way.
Nothing seems wrong to them.

However, for those people who picked up this book, something seems off.

There's another way out there.
There must be.

Limit Breaker

The body cannot fly.
I can flap my arms as much as I want, but that's not enough to elevate me above the ground.

The mind can fly.
There are no limits.
None.

What a time to be alive. The mind can defy gravity, and we have all the tools at our disposal.

For us to fly in the mind and look beyond the surface level, we just need to make curiosity work for us. Rather than directing it down, or not directing it anywhere at all, let us direct it towards the universe.

Let us feel unlimited.

To learn more about the mind, learn about the universe.
To learn more about the universe.... learn more about the mind.

That's growth mindset in a nutshell.

How can you possibly learn at infinite rates?
By learning in the first place.

Through the process of gaining more knowledge, there will be more opportunities to gain more wisdom. New information from others can be combined with past experiences. This leads to behavioral changes. Behavioral changes spark new knowledge which will fuel new thought waves.

I can keep going on and on...
The point is that you are developing into a Limit Breaker
before your very eyes.

A Limit Breaker is a person who sees no boundaries.
Simply 'challenges' to be shattered.

This is a person who knows no fear. Instead, you're a person
who makes light of situations. Not in a condescending way.
Instead, in a way that allows you to feel bold.

I was sad when Vinnie called out my younger self for
smirking. I thought he found the hole in the superpower I
deemed flawless.

Nowadays, I am happier than ever. Yes, I was making light of
the Hell Chamber, Vinnie. Because I viewed the Hell Chamber
to be a waste of time.

Still, I needed to participate. I was a member. If I'm going to
participate, do I do it with a bad attitude, or an empowering
one? The answer is obvious.

Read between the analogies, my friend.

If it is the nature of the mind to be curious, then what are you
going to do? Will you follow the rules of gravity, or will you
finally fly?

How this Book Works

I've lost count of how many times someone told me they bought my books because the covers looked cool. I put a lot of thought behind my covers.

I'm not a big fan of the saying, '*Never judge a book by its cover.*'
We can't help it.

Even though some of the best readings I've ever had were of the books with an awful front-end design.

For my books, the imagery that you **first** see is an extension of the book. It paints the narrative in the mind of the reader for what to expect.

The same people who initially bought the books for the cover ended up staying because of the content.

In the Limit Breaker, you will get the content in short story form. This book is a part of the *"101 Short Stories, Essays and Insights to Improve Communication Skills Series."*

All the books are unordered. You can pick up any of them and read along.

Likewise, all the short stories in this book are unordered. You can pick up any story and read whichever one resonates with you.

The content discussed in this book range from the variety of topics within soft skills. The intangibles.

Soft skills and communication skills are often interchanged.
Both phrases virtually mean the same thing.

I don't *only* believe in communication with others.
I believe in communication with yourself.
The stronger the communication with yourself, the more you
will be well equipped to deal with others.

In this book, you will learn about mindset, how to build a
tribe, outgrowing limiting beliefs, becoming fearless and
much more.

All topics which can build practical value in your life and
allow you to direct your curiosity towards the skies.

Certain insights will resonate with you more than others and
that's fine. Each one will target different desires and will
allow you to gain more perspective.

The stories are set up in a way where I talk about the lessons
learned through the lens of my life. This is my personal
journey in cultivating a Limit Breaker's mindset.

I aim to blend the arts and engineering. Certain talks are
simple with very informal language. However, the
engineering side sneaks in, with logical breakdowns and
analysis.

This is known as convergent and divergent thinking.

By placing your world view temporarily in my world view,
not only do you and I bond, but it also cheat codes the

learning process. You will imbibe certain lessons that took me years to understand, in a matter of seconds.

Bottom line, read the 101 stories as they suit you. Just know that each story is allowing you to defy gravity gradually until you SKYROCKET.

Unlocking your Inner Limit Breaker

The mind has infinite potential. It can learn for life. We aren't taught too much regarding how the mind works. I used to resent that lack of knowledge a while back. Nowadays, I am happy that was the case.

Confusion and curiosity work hand in hand.

When we are focused regarding something, we become more curious. Once we fulfill the curiosity, we find something new to be confused about.

In the real world, failures and confusion are good things if your intention was to defy gravity in the first place.

That's when losses turn into lessons and setbacks turn into setups.

We are living life in a way where the days should be viewed as chapters. Each day should be better than the last.

When the desire to be great is set, clarity will be a reward of its own.

The mind knows no limits.
Each story can take on infinite twists and turns.

The 101 short stories will enter your mind one way but will
subtly leave you in a different way.

Just like the imagination can envision whatever it desires.
Perception can be molded in any way that we can imagine.

Break limits.
Set new limits.
And break those again.

All these boundaries are a playground for you to lap one past
record after another. Even though the world has blinders on,
you can use that as an opportunity to fuel your rocket
further.

It only takes one Limit Breaker to inspire a generation of
winners to be.

Best wishes and enjoy the book.

How To Deal with Doubt

A hater points out your flaw & leaves it at that.
-No good intention.
A critic points out your flaw & gives you areas of
improvement.
-They have a good intention.

However, despite a critic being needed, they are still below
the totem pole of a creator.
-A creator is the goal, never the critic.

No child is like to their parents, 'Mom & dad, I want to be a
critic when I grow up!'
It just sort of happens.

Some creators have a critic mix to them. But the critic part is
only a side dish, not the main entree.

'Why does all this matter Armani?'
It matters because it gives a 360 degree look of the
ecosystem. It explains why even great people feel massive
doubt.

A creator's mindset is the top of the totem pole.

The creme de la creme. You're SUPPOSED to feel doubt. It's
something that is supposed to be expected.

When doubt is expected, fear is dissipated.

To this day, I still feel a lot of doubt when I have a presentation coming up. A part of me thinks, 'what if I forget the whole talk and make a fool out of myself?'

I thought the doubt goes away after speech 10. But no. I've given more than 50 speeches in my life & still have the same doubt.

Which is why nowadays, **I expect it.**
When I expect it, the narrative changes.

I'm not telling you to forget everything and just look out for the doubt. Instead, when or if doubt does show up, just be like, 'Oh it's you. Have a seat. Want some water?'

Your doubt is going to be like, *you're not scared of me??*
You can be like, 'no, I need you.'
This is when the internal tension melts.

I used to hate art growing up. Thought it was stupid.

As I matured, I realized the elegance & the elevated state of consciousness that it took to produce it.

The transition from a hater to appreciation happened. I was the same. But the awareness changed.

As consciousness rose, I learned how many of the fears experienced were created because I was fighting against something rather than accepting.

There was this guy named Michael Singler. He wrote a book called the Surrender Experiment.

Michael built a billion-dollar software company by surrendering to circumstances that he couldn't control.

It's normal to think that surrendering would cause him to feel powerless. Surprisingly, him letting go of what he couldn't control allowed him to feel more powerful.

Trying to remove doubt is like telling yourself never to think a thought again. That's a silly goal to chase in the first place. Instead, it's smarter to say:
'I am going for the peak, so doubts are normal. When I get them, I'll just acknowledge them, rather than trying to bury them.'
A suppressed emotion goes to the gym & comes back 10 times stronger.

Learn to flow. Eventually, what you don't fight leaves on its own.

'That doesn't make logical sense!!'

Emotional intelligence plays by different rules, bud. A brand-new language.

Doubt means you need to practice more & embrace more. Let the walls down. You're chasing the life of a creator. The road less taken.

1 out of 10 take this road.
That's why a creator will always be on the top of the totem pole.

4 Basics of Language

Acronyms make things easier. From afar, it just seems like letters and periods.

If you look closer, it's an intertwining of ideas.

One acronym that I was familiar with growing up
was **S.T.E.M.** It stands for Science, Technology, Engineering &
Mathematics. Each of the subjects played off each other.

As an engineering student, I learned a lot
about science, technology & math in my classes. 4 worlds met
under 1 domain.

Well, in the communications world, the same concept applies.
But in this world, it is:

R.L.S.W.
Reading, Listening, Speaking & Writing.

The 4 elements of language break down into those
components. They are seen as the macro level of
communication. The micro includes stuff like grammar, tone,
attention span etc.

Reading & listening are input skills.

This is when information is being inputted from the external
world to the internal world.

The best way to get good at this is by sharpening focus.

Writing & speaking are output skills.

This is when information is being outputted from the internal world to the external world.

The best way to get good at this is by staying consistent.

It really is as simple as that.

Just saying 'I am bad at communication' is vague and it puts the brain in a predicament. Very tough to get direction that way.

Your brain doesn't like complexity.
It likes simplicity.

Which of the 4 basics do you need to work on?
This question turns a hazy concept into clear one for the brain.

With consistency, this question takes up a life of its own & morphs into action. Poor communicator? Not anymore.

Outputs and inputs have been maximized. Now clear words pour out & understanding pours in. That's a modern renaissance man.

The Power of Symbols

There is an iconic image of Michael Jordan winning his first ever championship.

Before I bring it up, you may know what I am talking about. It's the picture of him holding a trophy closely & crying. It became an iconic photo for multiple 3 peats to come.

But if you are highly logical and objective, you may view the picture from a different lens. He is technically holding a material.

The trophy is golden, curved with a ball and a hoop. But it's still a material.

Why is it making him cry?

It's because of the symbol.

The mind loves symbols. Our entire world is based off symbols.

Picture shaking hands with someone. Why do you do that? That doesn't logically make sense.

Doesn't matter. It's a symbol for building rapport.

'Why are symbols needed?'
Symbols are needed for mental models.

Mental models allow the brain to think less so it can allocate brain power for other activities.

'Can you give me an example of another symbol?'
Sure. Your name.

Your name is a just a bunch of letters stringed together.
Imagine your life without a name.

People would need to wave their hands trying to get your
attention. They would probably only contact you if the
message was VERY important. This would cause you to lose
out on a TON of social connections.

It was Dale Carnegie who stated in 'How to Win Friends &
Influence People' that a person's name is the sweetest sound
in their world.

So yes, a string of letters is pretty damn important.

- o   The mind loves these constructs.
- o   The mind loves these mental models to make sense of
  the world.

During my engineering career, a lot of my classmates and coworkers were atheists.

I don't have anything personal against atheists, but I was
curious about their mental position.

Some of them were very well thought out. Others just blurted
out, *because I can't see a God!*

Either way, their minds ruled out the existence of an
intelligent creator.

However, what their mind didn't rule out was the role of
symbols in culture and to their personal lives.

The symbols could have been:

- o *Their engineering degree.*

- o *Their name.*

- o *A creative act.*

Whatever the case was, most of them had SOME thing of value for their symbol.

'What if I don't have a symbol?'
Then symbols will be assigned for you.

That's where the mainstream media often gets slick. They are highly intelligent with psychology. They understand that the human mind is naturally scattered & needs some sort of bullseye.

So, they will take up the role as the broadcasters of information. A supreme authority in your world.

If it's not the mainstream media, then it may be actors or actresses in Hollywood. I know certain parts of the world where they view their entertainment stars as deity's. Maybe even a sports figure.

Just know this...

The mind is looking for **something**. Some form of north star. Without it, its scatters away looking for answers.

When you feel like you have the right answer, you'll know. It's something that is hard to logically explain.

If you were to ask Michael Jordan why he was crying holding a material object, he wouldn't be able to logically explain it.

But remember...

Emotional intelligence isn't something that you logic yourself into. That leaves you with more questions than answers.

Emotional intelligence comes down to the **experience**. The only person that can experience your emotions is you.

Respect other people's symbols. It shapes a large part of their perception. Even if you don't agree with it, all good. They are the ones experiencing the feelings, not you.

Fall back on this one.

- o Do you find symbols to be important or a waste of time?
- o Do you have any symbols that you hold dearly to your heart?
- o How do the symbols in your life influence your behavior?

These are the bigger questions which surprisingly make you wake up from a blind world.

The Greatness of Linkin Park

When I was in the 5th grade, there was this girl named Valerie who sat next to me in class.

I had a crush on Valerie.

She was this brown-haired girl with braces who always wore some peculiar shoes. It was those skateboard shoes called Etnies.

The sole of those shoes wrote, *'I love Linkin Park.'*

I went home one day to Google what Linkin Park was. Found out that they were a band.

Perfect. Now I have conversation material for Valerie.

The next day, as a bunch of us were waiting in line for lunch, I go up to Valerie.

I was like:
Hey Valerie. You heard Linkin Park's new song? It's so good.

Valerie looked back at me in silence. She didn't say anything. A bunch of the people around us were waiting for her response but she wasn't saying anything.

Eventually, Valerie's friend asked her if she heard my question.

That's when Valerie blurts out, *'I can't talk to Armani. He's a nerd!'*

Everyone around me started laughing. Even my close friends. I was pissed & thought Valerie was a bitch.

Never talked to her again.

A few years went on by...

My cousin from Dubai came to visit me and my brother in West Palm.

I remember one day, he came into my room and said, *'hey make sure you are free on the third Saturday of May.'*

I asked him why?

He said Linkin Park was coming into town and that he bought me and my brother tickets to go.

Automatically, the memory of Valerie came up. I told him I didn't want to go. But he said it was too late, the tickets were already bought.
The day of the concert rolled around. It was called Projekt Revolution. I was there with a sour mood.

It was hot as shit. There was a bunch of bands that I never heard of.

Plus, I was a rap fan. My brother and cousin were the ones who liked rock.

As hours went on by, I was ready to go home. This was not fun.

However, there was no leaving. Linkin Park didn't perform
until night. As the hours flew on by, the
sunlight disappeared, and the moon showed its face.

Linkin Park was set to perform in 1 hour.

My cousin walked us to our seats. I thought we were going to
be sitting in the back around the grass area. But no, that
wasn't the case.

We had seats in the FRONT ROW.

We were the first ones there. Eventually, the seats began to
fill up and the host came on stage to announce the legendary
Linkin Park.

The lights shined.
The crowd erupted.
Then the beginning of the song 'Somewhere I Belong' began
to play.

Chester Bennington, Mike Shinoda & the other members came
out & the crowd ERUPTED.

Even though I was in a sour mood that whole day, something
had changed.

I finally let my guard down.

Something magical happened at that moment.
'What was that Armani?'
I was witnessing greatness.

Linkin Park sounds just as amazing in person as they do on
their records. The level of passion that the band

performed with was something to witness. From the
lead singer all the way to the drummer. It was elegance at its
finest.

Even though I was a rap fan, I had to give respect where
respect was due.

Sometimes when you witness greatness, you need to just shut
up and witness.

The reason that the media gets annoying is that they can't
ever witness. They love taking the beauty out of things.

Rather than appreciate greatness, they automatically go into
the comparison game.

Lebron is great.
Kobe is great.

'But who is better? More on this in the next segment.'

That sells, I get it. But it prevents you from discovering
your own greatness.

'How does someone else's greatness make me discover my
own?'
It gives perspective.

Being different gets a bad reputation.
But being different is chapter one of being legendary.

The unique thing about Linkin Park was that they had a
rapper in the rock band.

A few other bands were doing that at the time. But it wasn't
the norm. Mike Shinoda caught my attention, but Chester

Benington kept it (Rest in peace).

No one was born great. They had to put in tons of reps to get to where they are today.

So, when greatness appears, we are witnessing the
end product of years of work.

If you're astute enough, then you'll learn more from that performance than a lot of classes in formal education.

The real world is your school. People become great, but they often don't get acknowledgment for it until they die.

There's a beauty to celebrating someone's talent when they are alive. That will motivate others to become top tier in their field as well.

I didn't like Linkin Park until I couldn't stop loving them.

When I finally gave them a chance and bought their records, I noticed every song from Meteora and Hybrid Theory were fire.

Every song was fire?
That's not normal!

Look out for things that are not normal. Being prolific is the compass towards a legendary career.

Notice greatness before the masses turn it into a fad.

Those are the divine eyes.

Uncontrollable Anger

Orlando is not too *far* away *from* Tampa. The drive is roughly 1.5 hours away.

So, whenever a major news story happens in Orlando, I'll hear about it in Tampa. One of the major news stories involved a tragic murder.

A pastor *found* out his *wife* was sleeping with a church member. When he heard the news, he was livid & went to confront his *wife*.

As he went to confront his *wife*, he noticed she was with her brother. The brother protected his sister *from* the pastor's rage.

As the pastor left in anger, he said one thing to the brother. Which went something along the lines of 'promising to kill his sister.'

Which he unfortunately did.

This is a very popular pastor in the Orlando area with a cult like *following*. He was viewed as a prophet by his *followers*.

The Facebook pictures of him seemed colorful & *full* of life.

Contrast that with his *face* after his arrest. The pastor was now in court. He seemed shocked by what he had done. Knowing very well that he threw away his life, *forever*.

A life was lost, family in shambles & another life most likely
sentenced to life in prison. This began with uncontrollable
anger.

Blind rage is a thing.
It's something that you may not know about if you never
experienced it.

It's has a similarity with being blacked out from alcohol.
Where a person is capable of functioning despite a mind that
is in another realm.

- o   During blackout drunk, you do stuff that you regret.
- o   During blind rage, you do stuff that you regret.

Uncontrollable anger is fire. One of the worst ways to combat
fire is with more fire.

In the world of humans, anger is a sign to distance.
Which is harder than it seems.

The pastor was unable to distance. He instead, closed the
gaps. That's when chaos ensued.

'Why is distance a good fix for anger?'
Because of the brain structures.

**During anger, the amygdala overpowers the prefrontal
cortex.**
The prefrontal cortex is responsible for the logical faculties.
The amygdala is the fierce animal side.

Distance is powerful because as time passes, the amygdala

goes from survival instincts to cooling off.

Everything is not black & white in the world of humans. Some people are so livid by a situation where distance seems like the **last** option. It's hard as hell.

Still, it's one of the most effective strategies during moments of rage. Unfortunately, the pastor did not have the awareness or strategy to exercise the strategy.

Now his life is forever altered, along with his victim. Sad.
Emotions come & go.
Yet, the consequences can come & stay.

Unfortunately, it's dark times like this that remind us of the dark aspects of human nature.
Rest in peace.

The Story of The Fat Kid

Have you ever taken the time to look into jealousy?

We hear about the word & understand it is an emotion, but let's look a little deeper. The best way to understand the emotion is by taking a walk down memory lane.

23 years ago, I was living in Bangladesh. I remember going to school in Chittagong.

Well, there is one particular memory that sticks out.

This was my first day going to school. My mom & dad prepped me, but I wasn't ready for it.

At the time, I was just a trouble making kid who wanted to hang out with his friends & play hide n seek. Your boy didn't want to sit in some classroom and learn.

I remember when I got into class, I was immediately alarmed by how small it was. A crowded room of kids my age, hot room & poor lighting.

To make matters worse, almost all the chairs were taken...
Except one.

There was one chair open next to the wall right by this one kid. This kid was fat as hell.

Me sitting there would require me to be sandwiched between the wall and this fellow. But I had no choice. So, I sat down right next to him.

Immediately, I could feel this guy's presence. He smelled like shit & was very loud. Anytime he would move his body, he would make a grunting noise.

What was more annoying was that this kid kept rubbing shoulders with me. I was not only disgusted, but a very annoyed.

Throughout the day, I was showing all the signs of annoying body language. I was sighing, rolling my eyes, & doing some grunt moves as well.

But this kid had no clue.
He was just carrying on & behaving like a pig.

What **really** irked me was my teacher. She was some lady in her 30s who kept circling around the class.
You would expect her to notice how I annoyed I was, right?

Nah...
Exact opposite.

She kept coming to the fat dude and kept asking him how his day was going. She kept inquiring if he was okay or if he needed anything.

By the time she would pass me, she would simply smile & keep it moving.

Huh?? What kind of clown universe is this?
I AM the one getting agitated by this fat clown!

And here you are, acting like I don't even exist. Whatsup with that?

Needless to say, I was very JEALOUS of this fat kid.

Few months went by & I eventually ended up switching seats. But my jealousy for the kid never went away.

There was one time he tried talking to me after class, however, I completely ignored him. Didn't like the guy whatsoever.

Someone told me that he may have had a medical issue, which was why the teacher kept checking up on him.

But my primal brain was so jealous that I completely neglected to follow up. I continued to live in my bubble that this kid was my enemy.

Unique, isn't it?

The emotion of jealousy was never taught. No one formally told me to give this kid the cold shoulder. I just did it because I felt the emotion & reacted.

23 years later, I went back to that memory to make sense of it.

Why did I behave like that?
   o   It's because I was jealous of the kid.

Why was I jealous of the kid?
   o   Because he got attention from my teacher while I was ignored.

The more I made sense of that incident, the more that I was able to learn something about jealousy.

If you want to leverage it, you must clarify it.

My kid self simply reacted to the emotion & treated it like it was reality.

My adult self aimed to go thru the layers until the emotion could be explained with rationale.

You can do the same when you are feeling jealous.

Simple Jealousy Formula:

1. You feel an emotional response of jealousy.
2. You need to keep questioning the emotional response until you have your aha moment.

Example:

Why am I jealous?

  o   Because I want attention.

Why do I want attention?

  o   Because I want to feel important.

Why can't you make yourself feel important, why do you need someone else to do that for you?

  o   Aha! Good point!!

Jealousy will give you a lot of your eureka moments. In the level up world, we use jealousy as a compass & a vehicle for growth.

Compass: it helps identify a weak spot in your life.

Vehicle: you place attention to that weak spot & make magic happen.

Unfortunately, many people never grow past their kid self. They simply see a fat kid taking up their space, get ignored by their teacher & let jealousy corrode them from within.

Well, maybe not that exact situation, but you get the point!

Ask yourself:
What have you been holding onto?

Path 1: Have you been reacting to jealousy (*giving the fat kid the cold shoulder*).
Or
Path 2: Have you been responding to the jealousy *(asking why questions until you get to the root cause?).*

Your response & behavior will represent your emotional intelligence and your emotional intelligence will determine your level of happiness.

So, pick wisely.

Michael Jordan Mentality

Michael Jordan is known as the greatest basketball player of all time. A mentally tough athlete who has the championships to his legacy. 6 out of 6 in the finals.

He's a winner, no denying that.

Even though Michael Jordan is viewed as a winner on the court, he has gotten his fair share of backlash. One of the biggest criticisms of MJ is that he doesn't talk enough about social issues.

That's one thing people point out when they want to criticize him. They say he lacks character.

Plenty of people fall for this narrative too. But if you look closer, the notion that he 'lacks character' is subjective.

I have a different perception on why he stays out of politics.

Guys like MJ don't see isolated events. They realize a lot of things as connected.
As in... You miss one practice, then who knows. You may miss another...and another...

These people see everything in patterns & interconnections.
MJ is a systems thinker.

When the media tries to get a response out of him for something politically related, he often hesitates.
'Why?'
Because a political opinion is nuanced, not black & white.

There are a lot of variables that one should be aware of if they want to offer a **well thought** out opinion on politics. Not just a knee jerk response.

They think that if you offer 1 opinion, then all your problems are over. However, that's rarely the case.

There are 2nd order, 3rd order, 4th order effects for these types of decisions The more complex a system becomes, the more the little things matter.

That's why you see so many celebrities Also, factor in the variable that MJ is an influential figure. He's not just sharing an opinion. But his opinion has the power to change a lot of beliefs.

MJ is aware of his influence.
He is also aware of providing opinions on topics that he is not well informed on.

Most people will be like, 'just offer an opinion & call it a day!' That's how most people think.
often going mad.

Their social system became way too complex. And their agents, PR reps, family & friends kept adding & adding to their system.

Eventually, something as small as providing a political opinion has a chain effect.

This isn't to say that celebrities should avoid offering political opinions. But more so to evaluate why particular celebrities sit out in the public eye & contribute in the private eye.

Plus, MJ doesn't owe shit to anyone.

The mainstream media tries to pull their virtue card out like he owes them something. With a little media literacy, it's easy to see that getting opinions from influential figures can easily become weaponized.

If the opinion fits their agenda, then the opinion will be used as credibility against their opposition. If the opinion doesn't fit their agenda, then the character of the opinion holder will be questioned.

I give props to people who are in the political field and make a contribution and props to those who aren't in the field but take their time to be well informed before talking.

But **forcing** someone to have an opinion is idiotic.

Typically, that's why people talk so much nowadays. Especially on topics that they don't know diddly squat about.

There used to be a time when saying, *'I don't know much about the topic to answer that'* was seen as commendable. Nowadays, many move different.

This talk was not about Michael Jordan really. It was more so about understanding how systems thinkers operate.

When someone is continuously behaving a certain way, it's because they are consciously or subconsciously processing a bunch of interconnections from their life.

It has very little to do with you.

Remember that the next time you are interacting with someone. Typically, the more aware you become, the more systems that you begin to think in.

The words turn into pictures & the pictures turn into movies.

How to Become a Better Storyteller

Warren Buffet.

He is known for a few things.

You know a person is known for things when you can use words to describe him.

What words come to mind when thinking of Warren Buffet?
- o   Investor.
- o   Invest in yourself.
- o   Compound effect.
- o   Read.
- o   Benjamin Graham.

Let's zone in on the final line. Benjamin Graham. The author of the Intelligent Investor.

I read the book, Intelligent Investor during a time when I didn't know much about money. I was just an average high school kid who wanted to get rich.

Due to my lack of experience, I picked up the book to read it. *Thought it was super boring and put it for years.*

However, the curiosity of investing was still there. Rather than reading books, I decided to read a few blogs on the subject. That's when I saw the word **commodities** popping up left and right.

A few years later, I saw Robert Kiyosaki, the author of Rich

Dad Poor Dad come through to Tampa. He used an incredibly unique term for commodities. He called them, *God's Money.*

He said gold and silver were here before we were here, and gold and silver will be here after we die.

'I invest in God's money,' he said with pride.

'Stocks, bonds and all the other papers stuff are simply a derivative of Gods money,' he said in disgust.

That phrase was unique. God's Money. It allowed me to see gold & silver with new eyes. The world of commodities made more sense.

Commodities are raw goods. Products are raw goods which have been manufactured into something of use.

'Glad you're giving this walk down memory lane. But what the hell does this have to do with storytelling?'

There is an analogy between the world of money & the world of words, my friend.

You see....
Your experiences are raw goods.
- o   *Picture silver found in the land.*

Your stories are your experiences manufactured into a product.
- o   *Picture the silver that is now a watch.*

This allowed me to see the invisible world of words.

It's not easy to think of a speech topic. Or a topic for a blog article. Or even a topic for emails.

It's easy to over think.
So, let's simplify it.

Are you mining Gods Money, **aka experiences** which they already possess?

- o   God's money in the outside world are gold and silver.
- o   God's money in the insider world are your memories.

It's easy to tell stories when you talk about your own life. What have you been through?

There are 365 days in a year. Therefore, writing 365 stories is light work.

Bottom line is, you have the commodities, aka experiences. That's not the issue.

The question is, how many of those commodities are you turning into products?
Aka, stories.

This is also excellent news because perception is malleable. By walking down memory lane, it's easier to change narratives of negative memories.

Which is why transformative art is a popular field.
'What is that?'
Transformative art is when the user creates art to transform themselves from within.

Stories have power because words serve as a magnifying glass for the mind. You get to choose where you want that magnifying glass pointed.

This allows you to extract meaning from the experiences which you overlooked.

If you decide to share it, then who knows, others may be able to learn from your meaning.

The summary of how to become a better storyteller is by:

1. Extracting the commodities from the mines. Experiences from your past.
2. Manufacture the commodities into goods. Turn the experiences into a tale.

Experiences + Narrative = Story.

Rinse and repeat, you'll feel the transformative effects of storytelling in no time.

Leverage Emotional Intelligence to Leverage Creativity

You know what I noticed?

'What?'

A lot of artists of the past & present were weird.

- o *Vincent Van Gogh cut off his ear.*
- o *Eminem practically did every drug in the book.*
- o *Edgar Allan Poe.... well, don't even get me started on him.*

Despite being very weird, they produced masterpieces that will outlast them.

Although their personalities were out of whack, it didn't deter them from producing. Heck, their weird personalities may have been the missing puzzle piece to their greatness.

You see, although logic is great & needed in your lifestyle to maintain structure, it is not the best tool for innovation. **Innovation requires creativity.**

'How do you define creativity?'

I define creativity as being *weird with structure.*

Therefore, all of those artists may have been onto something.

Have you ever wondered why it is during your dark times in

which create the best?

It's because of one major element....

Emotional pain produces a genius.

'Huh??'

If you look up the term genius, it is someone who has supreme intellectual OR creative abilities.

With intellectual aspect, it is easy to measure. Check out someone's IQ score & deduce whether or not they fall into the genius scale. With the creative part, it is very difficult to measure.

Only *you* can measure it.

The reason that emotional pain is good for creativity is due to thought frequencies.

When you feel emotional pain, your body is generating internal energy. With the energy, you can go into destruction or production mode.

- o   Destruction Mode = doing drugs, getting drunk, partying away the pain.

In the destruction phase, the human uses external stimulants to numb the internal energy.

- o   Production Mode = making art, writing stories, creating videos etc.

In the production phase, the human uses internal energy to produce external masterpieces.

One is emotionally unintelligent; one is emotionally intelligent. I'll let you guess which is which.

In the production phase, as you harness the energy within rather than numb it, something magical happens....

Your brain starts thinking in new thought patterns.

Rather than the traditional logical thoughts, you start thinking in different wavelengths. The frequency is much higher.
The higher the frequency, the higher the innovation.

Emotional intelligence comes down to understanding that:
Emotions = Feelings + Perception

Get to a point where you can dictate the perception at will. Then leverage the feelings to think innovatively. Once innovation has been sparked, then release it on the creative outlet of your choice.

You were a genius all along. It just requires leveraging emotional intelligence to unleash it.

- o   If you are going through a good portion in life, then enjoy it.
- o   If you are going through a dark portion in life, then leverage it.

Get to a point where you see win - win.
'Does that mean I can never be sad?'
Nah, be sad when you are sad. Just don't let it destruct your behavior.

Use your internal energy to produce.
Join the top 3% & become immortal.

How To Deal with Stupid People

Let me share a story about a difficult day. It all dealt with the internet. The story begins at 10 am in the morning.

Around 10 in the morning, my internet stopped working. This was bad considering I had a client call at 11 am.

Bad start considering this was going to be my **first call** with this client.

After trying to start my internet for the next 45 minutes, I had no luck. Decided to go to a Starbucks to take the Skype call.

By the time it's 11 am, I began the call.
Automatically, it started off bad.

The Starbucks was extra loud for some strange reason. There were multiple groups chilling by me who were feeling extra energetic. Laughing & practically screaming.

This made it very difficult to hear my client & vice versa.

The call was going very poorly & at that point, I decided it's best that we rescheduled.

By the time I get back home, I call the internet provider to see what went wrong with the internet. Some lady named Ashley picked up.

You ever had that moment when you could just tell the service was going to go poorly?

Well, that was the case for me on this particular day. Ashley had this very rude tone & I could tell this was going to be a difficult conversation.

She did some research and said there was no outage in my neighborhood. But for some strange reason, I was the only house in the vicinity whose internet wasn't working.

Luckily, 3 years in the IT industry signaled to me that a simple node restart from her end would have resolved the issue. But Ashley was hesitant in trying that.

'That's not something I can do from my end, sir. Try unplugging your modem & router' Ashley said.

I knew that wouldn't do much but played along anyway.

After an hour of unplugging & restarting, I was getting agitated.

Ashley decides it would be best if she creates a ticket for a service agent to come & see what's wrong. She said someone would be at my place by Wednesday afternoon.

Mind you, it is Saturday at this point. She is expecting me to go 4 days without an internet connection.

Well, something like this happened 3 months before when I first moved into this neighborhood. When it was expected to take so long to send help over, I asked if there was any other way. The agent at that time said he could upgrade the status of the ticket to expedite the issue. Which he did.

I asked Ashley to see if she could bump up the status of the ticket, since this causing an issue.

However, Ashley was adamant.
She said it was simply not possible.

I told her it was possible considering it had been done 3 months ago.

But at this point, her ego had gotten involved, so she dug her heels deeper in the ground trying to be stubborn.
I was getting visibly annoyed. No way in hell was I going to wait 4 days to get my internet back.

I raised my voice & told her to stop wasting my damn time. Either restart the node or upgrade the status of the ticket.

She refused.
I told her to transfer me to her manager.
She did.

By the time I was transferred to the manager, you could tell Ashley had filled him in on the story. So, he came on the call pretty defensive, basically reiterating what Ashley had said.

Once again, I let him know about how my ticket was upgraded a few months back, so I knew what I was asking for was not impossible. If he couldn't do that, then he needs to restart the network node. Either case, I am not hanging up without my internet being resolved **today**.

After having a 45-minute standoff, this guy finally decided to restart the network node.

'I'm sure it won't work sir, but since you keep insisting, I'll give it a try,' said the manager.

Guess what?
Surprise surprise...

After he restarted the node, my internet connection had come back on. It only took 3.5 hours to get to this point.

By the time my internet began functioning, you could tell the manager was embarrassed. A customer had shown him how to do his own damn job.

I said, 'thank you for your time' and hung up.
You could tell he was pretty surprised I didn't go on a 'told you so' spree.

I didn't care about being right. I cared about my internet coming back, so I could get back to work.

What can you learn from this story?

To begin, I want to be clear that I had gotten REAL pissed at both Ashley & her manager. I raised my voice & dropped a few curse bombs in the mix.

That's me being transparent. I am just like any person out there. I lose my cool at times too.

Now with that being said.

Do I regret what I did?
Absolutely not.

It was clear as day that Ashley & her manager were just in it for a paycheck.

- o   They don't give a fuck about their customers.
- o   They give a fuck about their precious little egos.

By the time I went on Google reviews to see what other customers thought, let's just say the average 1.4-star review from a 1000+ customers spoke volumes.

I read Dale Carnegie's book 'How to Win Friends & Influence People' a while back.

In his book, he preaches being patient all the time & gently asking questions till others can formulate the right decision on their own.

Is that wrong?
No.
But is it always practical?
Not in my opinion.

In my eyes, sometimes you need be human and let your anger let them know you mean business.

Time is money.

Ashley & her bumass manager would not give a fuck if I had 4 days wasted.

Sometimes, you need to show some force.
I call this 'anger with intent.'

Being angry for the sake of being angry can create a loose cannon. But being angry with an intent is a rare move that can be executed in certain circumstances.

Just a quick disclaimer, this move is risky, so you need

to know the right time to use it.

'When do you think is the right time?'
I think it is the right occasion when time is on the line & you have no other choice.

In my story, time was on the line. If the anger with intent didn't work, then the technician would have come on Wednesday anyways.

This may be an unpopular opinion among many people who talk about communication skills.

I think anger with purpose can get lazy clowns to take some action & be more mindful on how to do their damn job.

There are a lot of personalities in the social world. Most times, it's smart to ignore & keep composure.

However, anger is a move that I believe can be leveraged in **rare** cases if it is **absolutely** needed.

If you don't feel comfortable doing the move, then no need to force it. Just do what you think is best.

I wanted to share this story to introduce the anger with intent concept.

If it's not a phrase yet, then I'll go ahead and patent it.

The Global Village

The world has shrunk. Technology has allowed the world to break down the walls. We are more interconnected than ever in terms of relaying a message.

What's crazy is that Marshall McLuhan created the term 'Global Village' in the 60s.

The SIXTIES.

This is before the internet, Google, Facebook, or any other social media for that matter.

He knew that media technologies were going to make the world shrink. He saw what many had no clue about.

2 years ago, I had a kid named Steve hit me up on Facebook messenger. I was thinking, who is this guy?
I don't know a Steve.

Then he said, 'Bro, we used to be best friends in the 2nd grade.'
That's when I paused.

Steve...

Steve...
Steve Barauntus??

Whoa!!! It was the same Steve that I knew decades ago.

Steve and I were best friends in the 2nd grade. We would partner up for projects, have inside jokes & hang out. Thought we would be friends into adulthood.

'What happened?'
He moved to Switzerland. It was sudden too. He told me on
the last day of 2nd grade that he would not be returning.

Thought we were never going to see each other. Thought it
was a chapter closed in terms of friendship.

Until Facebook happened.

Somehow, he was able to remember how to spell my big last
name 'Chowdhury' and find me. Chowdhury is the Smith's of
Bengali's. Extremely popular last name.

You probably have an interesting story like this too.
Where technology allowed you to reconnect, maintain a
connection or meet someone from a different side of the
world.

It's as though they are living right next door. But nah, they
are MILES & MILES away.

Some of this stuff would have been considered voodoo by our
ancestors. Not anymore. Technology is still in the baby
phases. The best is yet to come.

Some people have a sinister view of technology. They think
it's the reason for poor attention spans.

Nah..
People are responsible for poor attention spans.
Technology is just a tool.

Millions of emails, tweets, blogs are being uploaded every
day.

All words relaying a message.

If you want to be a confident communicator, thrive offline, yes. But understand how the game is played online.

Me and you are friends at this point. Yet, we have never physically met.

Marshall McLuhan wasn't joking when he said we will be living in a Global Village.

Understand how the technology works so you don't become victim to it.

You can't control what you can't understand.

The best way to understand it is to see how you use communication technology in your day-to-day life. **Bring conscious awareness to it.**

After hearing the term 'Global Village' (which you may have never heard of until now) & along with the story of Steve, you'll probably be looking at communication technology differently.

Hopefully.

The Power of Consistency

In the summer of 2012, my good friend Sam and I decided that we were going to invest in the p90x workout program. It's a 90-day home workout program.

At the time, both of us had been in year 2 of our fraternities. After all the house parties, we both had gained weight. Time to commit to the program and get shredded!

There were some limiting beliefs though. I did not think that brown people had the genetics to get ripped.

He was Indian & I am Bengali. Despite these doubts, we decided to commit.

The first workout was tough.

We were so out of shape. The program had us doing burpees & all these jumping exercises. Felt like throwing up. And then we did...

After that workout, I didn't know how I was going to continue for 89 more days.

In the program, Tony Horton (the host) says to make sure you take pictures everyday of your transformation. That'll make sure you don't quit. Sure Tony, that's a good idea!

We kept the process going.

Month 1 was tough, but we got through it.
Month 2 began.

Apparently, month 1 was the warmup session. And month 2 is when it starts to kick off.
Huh??

You're telling me this month was going to be harder??
Oh boy.

We both pushed ourselves to keep it going. By month 2, we both started to get lazy.
'Any idea why?'
Yes.

As I was looking at the progress pictures, I didn't see a lick of improvement. Actually, it looked like I was getting fatter.

Here I was dieting, getting my 8 hours of sleep, and doing these hectic workouts. To only get fatter??

By the end of month 2, we both decided to have a do over for this month. Sam and I half assed the 30 days & we needed to be serious. So now it was p -120x.

Let's keep it going.

We kept pushing. Staying with the routine and putting in our reps. Eventually, Sam caved on the diet part. He worked out but stopped eating right.

At this point, for me, it was becoming muscle memory. The process was no longer too difficult. However, I was getting irked that I wasn't seeing the 6 pack yet.

By month 3 though, things began to change.

My body started to feel different, internally. Anytime I would eat (the same meals) I would feel hungry again very quickly. As if the metabolism sped up.

I started to **feel** different.

At this point, I became aware of a big mistake I was making. My bodybuilding classmate told me I was drinking TOO much water. Told me if I drank 3 liters, then a lot of my water weight fall off.

And looky looky...

I followed his advice for a week & there it was. Abs staring back at me in the mirror.

3.3 months of frustration later, it felt like the abs came out of nowhere. There was still room for improvement. But at least now the output (the pictures) was catching up to the input (work ethic).

It was due to consistency.

It is a similar phenomenon in so many fields. You and your buddy (or you alone) decide you are going to pick up a new habit.

In the first few weeks, you don't notice anything. Heck, it seems to be getting worse!

I don't know who made the 21 days to form a habit rule, but that has rarely been the case for me.

For me, its 3 months or bust.
Better to shoot for 6 months.
It shows that you genuinely want it.

Picking up a new habit is your body going through an inner transformation. Neurons are wiring and firing in brand new ways and the nervous system is feeling a ton of stress.

However, the human is a magnificent creature. One capable of ADAPTING.

If you know that you are doing everything correctly, then just be patient. Don't have the mindset that my buddy and I had on month 2. Where we were physically showing up to the workouts but were mentally absent.

P-90x workouts used to be an hour long. Nowadays, it's 30 minutes. Which is much better.

It's easy to be consistent when the workload is broken down into manageable portions. This warms up the brain in small doses while priming it to keep showing up.

These micro habits start to build up. That's how I built the ArmaniTalks brand.

I was never a writer.

My English teacher would always give me Cs in the class. She just didn't give me an F because she was a sweet lady.

I learned to write by tweeting. The smallest fraction of writing that you can imagine. Tweeted everyday AT LEAST once.

After a few months, momentum kicked in.
 These micro tweets led to:
-100s of blogs.
-Multiple books.

-Hundreds of emails.

Those tiny tweets turned into 50,000+ tweets at the time of writing this. That's the power of tiny.

Consistency turns little waves into a tsunami.

After a while, you can't stop even if you wanted too. Good or bad.

Why Someone Doesn't Forgive You

'Armani, I apologized, all good, right?'
Not always.

There are 2 reasons someone will not forgive you:
1. *It's too LATE to apologize.*
2. *It's too DEEP to apologize.*

Let's talk about both.

Some people don't forgive because it's too late.
The grace period of the apology has passed.

They wonder:
'What took you so damn long?'
The fact that it took so long registers negatively to their mind.

They want to pay you back by not accepting the apology, so they are on the higher state of power.

Other times, they just moved on.
Example:
Let's say you cheated on your high school sweetheart and now she is healed & married with kids. Your apology may seem like a nuisance. They are over the drama & don't want to invite that energy back into their life.

The second reason people don't accept an apology is because

it's too deep.

I've seen those videos in the courthouse where the parents forgive their kid's killer. The killer apologized and the parents forgave due to core beliefs.

But let's be real.
That's not always the norm.

I'm sure there are many more parents who will want the killer to rot no matter how flowery the apology is.

Why?
Because the act of hurt is too deep. You don't get your kid back.

Now all situations may not be that extreme. But we need to realize one main thing:
The person who you victimized is evaluating the DEPTH of the act from their lens, not yours.
Another example...
Let's say you forgot your wedding anniversary.

It may not mean too much to you. You think:
'I remembered the other 22 years. Who cares if I missed one?'

But for your wife, it may register as a deep one.

Anyways, these are all examples.
The 2 core principles are that people don't forgive for time or depth.

When you realize this, choosing the next move is on you.

It's not easy to apologize & not be forgiven. It's kind of like
watching a movie that leaves you off in a cliffhanger, with no
part 2. Feels weird.

'So what do I do?'
You just need to take the loss and learn from it.
Social skills are a constant refining process.

We probably have done a lot of things that doesn't warrant
forgiveness because our younger self just didn't know any
better.

Give yourself a pat on the back for admitting that you were in
the wrong, then gracefully take the loss.

This sort of stuff builds character. It's not wise to force
someone to take an apology by incessant begging. That can
lead to short term resolutions.

Some people fake apologies.
Some fake forgiveness.

They pretend to forgive, only to hold the poor actions over
you in the future. So, if that's the box you want to open, then
go for it. From my experience, it's a headache that's rarely
worth it.

Learning to take a loss says a lot about a person.
You can argue that it is impossible to build character without
learning the art of taking a loss.
'Did you just call taking a loss an art?'
That, I did.

Thick Skin = Remedy For All

Cocky or confident?
Serious question.
What is the difference?

To the untrained eye, the 2 can seem the same.
When looking closer, there is a difference.

For cocky, the person is externally motivated.
For confident, the person is internally motivated.

A cocky person wants approval. Something about their moves seem off. Their moves don't seem congruent to the interaction at hand.

The cocky person wants you to like them.
The confident person does not care if you like them or not.

The cocky person in a deep sense, does not like themselves. While the confident person in a deep sense, does like themselves.

With this line of thinking, we can apply similar frameworks to the difference between bragging & promotion.

It can seem similar to the untrained eye.
But to the trained eye, the 2 are different.

In context to bragging, it rarely provides value. It has an

essence of showing off & talking in a string of accomplishments.

But with promotion, there is value that is provided. Another party is CAPABLE of winning if the promotion is done correctly.

Imagine you are about to go to a networking event. Right before you are about to head to the event, your toilet stops working. You're running late. So you decide you'll deal with this issue once you get back.

You go to the event.

As you are about to enter, the host says you are not supposed to DIRECTLY ask anyone about their profession. If they tell you, that's one thing, but you can't directly ask.

So, you decide to get slick with it.

You start giving HINTS that you're looking for a plumber, hoping that someone will refer you to a plumber or come out as being one.

A lot of people pick up the clues but are too humble to say anything.

However, one person realizes your clue, comes out as a plumber, talks about their credentials & offers to help.

In this case, you're ecstatic! You went to the event & now got your plumbing issue resolved as well.

In this case, due to promotion, TWO parties were able to win.

-The plumber was able to close a deal.
-You got your toilet fixed.

That's what promotion breaks down to:
Is there a POTENTIAL for giving value?

With bragging, you can somehow accidentally give value. Someone shy may like an overly confident swag. Others may find this boaster entertaining.

With Conor McGregor, the UFC fighter, he was able to make a lot of money bragging about his success. But when looking closer, it was more than that.

What seemed like bragging to the outside world was value for his family & organization.
Conor needed to sell his fights.

In the fight game, it's hard to become a superstar by just fighting. A superstar is born by fighting AND charisma.

Trash talking is an art in boxing & UFC. That's why names like Muhammad Ali, Floyd Mayweather and Conor McGregor are remembered.

Due to Conor's '*bragging*,' he was able to make a lot of money for his family and help turn the UFC into a billion-dollar empire.

It all comes down to context at the end of the day.

Being able to read context is born through judgement. A person develops judgment by putting themselves in situations where they had success & where they had failure.

Bragging in most contexts is a low ROI act, because it isn't necessarily providing value and it sparks resentment in a lot of people.

I said, most contexts, not all contexts.

Promotion in a lot of contexts is perceived as bragging, when done with a poor delivery or delivered to someone who hates ANY sort of promotion.

The intent is correct, but the audience just doesn't want to hear it.

With blurry responses like this, a part of you may be thinking:
Then what's the point of it all? Even if I mean well, I may be perceived incorrectly.

Welcome to the social world.

That's why taking purposeful action to cultivating a thick skin is one of the BEST things to do for your present & future.

A thick-skinned person knows that misinterpretations can happen, but they move purposefully in the social jungle anyways.

With thick skin, contexts present themselves.
Understanding psychology & emotional intelligence deepens with a thicker skin.

It's when easier to spot WHY someone is bragging.
- o   Is this person insecure?

o   Is this like a Conor McGregor situation, where the bragging is actually a form of promotion?

o   Am I being too closed off? Maybe this guy isn't bragging at all. Maybe I'm just jealous of this guy?

This is a 4D understanding of social intelligence. A person with thin skin just isn't able to think in depth like this. They are black & white thinkers.

Notice...
The external world was better understood by first working on the internal world.
Thick skin is something within our control.

There are a lot of platitudes out there. Like:
"You can't control what happens to you. You can only control the response."

Hearing those platitudes is one thing. But realizing that insight on your own & being pleasantly surprised that someone made a platitude on it is something completely different.

Build thick skin.
Keep working on that.
Wear goggles that allow you to perceive situations differently.

Good moment? Great.
Bad moment? Great. My skin just got tougher.

Condition the mind to begin thinking like this.
Practice is king.

Along with humor, thick skin is a superpower in the game of life. It's what allows you to become strong.

Strength is the best thing you can do for yourself & the world. Temporary weakness happens to the best of us. But being weak in terms of character is the most selfish thing you can do.

Thick skin is the best long-term strategy out there.

It's the best way to allow the internal to influence the external. It's the best way to build awareness.

Most importantly, it's the best way to know why events that don't make sense now, *one day will.*

Less is More: Social Edition

We have heard the phrase: 'less is more.'
This phrase can be used in different parts of our life.

There is a Walmart in Tampa, one of the small ones. This is a great place to go for grocery shopping. It's not like the other big Walmart's where you need to wait 20 minutes to find parking.

Nice, small & efficient.

One day, I notice this Walmart hired a guy who stands near the shopping carts outside. He is a guy in his 60s, I believe, and his job is to separate the shopping carts & hand them to each customer.

Strange.

They didn't have this guy before.
So why now?

After this gentleman was hired, I noticed him struggling to separate each shopping cart. Since he was struggling, he was making a big line wait around the area.

Once again.
Strange.
Why even have this position?

Before this guy was working in the shopping cart area, everything was going fine. Each customer got the cart at their own pace & went about their day.

But by having this gentleman as a middleman, there was an impedance being formed.

Not hating on him. However, this was a case of adding components which did not need to be added. That added level of variability in a nonlinear system, led to a roadblock. **Plummeting efficiency.**

This is how it works with social skills as well.

We are all the artists of our life. It's crucial for an artist to have AT LEAST 1 rule.

Doesn't really matter what the rule is. It's important to have it.
Why?
Because then you form a nonnegotiable.

Through this nonnegotiable, it's easier to spot when you are getting off track. This allows you to say 'no' much faster.

One thing that I was not initially expecting as I was growing my ArmaniTalks business was how much advice I would be getting from all directions.

It feels like every day, someone is trying to sell me something new. I respect the hustle. But I don't need most of what is being pitched to me.

If I said yes to everyone, then my life would get too messy.
My message would get diluted.
And I would be like Walmart hiring a guy to just slow things down.

I don't like saying no to people. However, I do realize it's a
skill that needs to be mastered.
This is why it's crucial for an artist to have that #1 rule
minimum.

In the mid-2000s, Dave Chappelle was the butt of all jokes.

It's easy to forget that dark chapter in Dave's life because of
how he bounced back so gracefully.
But in mid 2000s, everyone was laughing at him for not
renewing another season of the Chapelle's Show.

He walked away from millions of dollars.

He said no to the big bucks & mainstream success to move to
Africa. Super surprising back then.

When he came back a few years later, he did an interview
explaining why he did what he did. Only problem was that
the interview was extremely cryptic.

If you paid attention to his body language & the way he was
talking, it was clear that he did not have his ONE BIG rule.
Causing him to be pulled in too many directions.

**Less is more in the social skills world because inviting a
human in is capable of infinite disorder.**

'Infinite? Okay, now you are exaggerating.'
No, I am not.
Infinite.

People are not linear creatures.

1 + 1 does not equal 2.
In a nonlinear world:
1 + 1 = ?

That question mark is why the artist should be wary of giving everyone their time.

That's not to say that being polite is bad. Being polite is good.

Having plenty of acquaintances is good.
But having a *few friends* is smart.

- o   Acquaintances are surface level connections.
- o   Friends are deep level connections.

It's one thing if you are strictly a consumer.
But if you are a producer in **any** facet of your life, the mind is king.

The mind must be made a priority.

Remember this:
With humans, no one is automatically valuing your time. It doesn't mean they are disrespecting it either. They are just behaving in a neutral way.

It's up to the artist to set the boundaries before things get out of hand. Before bursts of Dave Chappelle from mid 2000s happens to you.
Or if you start creating too many roadblocks like the shopping cart man.

The 'less is more' rule is often learned the hard way.

Hopefully, it's a lesson that is learned at one point or
another.

In some worlds, more may be more.
But with humans, that is rarely the case.

The Awkward Networker

-For a shy or an introverted person, networking seems very daunting.
-For an extroverted person, networking seems very daunting.

Lesson?
It doesn't matter what your personality type is, the act of networking can be a tad bit weird at times.

But why?
The weirdness comes from a lack of understanding.

I remember when I landed my first ever engineering job, my manager pulled me to the side and said:
*'Armani. If you ever want to become a somebody in this company, then you **need** to network. You need to shake hands with the right people.'*

As an eager 23-year-old, I was excited to put his advice into execution.

For the next few weeks, I went to tons of networking events. Found the higher ups, sucked up to them & was desperately hoping that they liked me.

But you know what I noticed?
'What?'
There were tons of other 23-year old's doing the same strategy as me.

I ended up being involved in an interaction with 3 other managers & my good friend Jon.

As Jon and I were talking in the conversation, we were both being completely fake. Both of us knew each other for years! But in this interaction? Both of us seemed unrecognizable to one another.

Years later, I understand why networking felt so weird.

It was because Jon & I were coming from a place of lower value. And when we came from a place of lower value, we tried to take before we gave.

Jon & I were both kissing their ass because we thought we would get ahead. By thinking that we were going to get ahead, we exited the present moment & began operating with an end game in mind.

This made us enter each interaction with an attitude of desperation. We were both the 'nice guys' of networking world.

Believe it or not, you may fall into this boat too.

'Nah dude, I don't kiss anyone's ass. Not my style.'
Okay. But are you that person who passes out their business cards like they pass out flyers?

'Um, yea.'
Well, then you are coming from a place of desperation. You are entering the interaction to take.

It's time to flip the mindset.
There are frameworks for networking.

'So, what is the secret bro??'

Provide 3x more value than you take.

Give so much that it makes them feel awkward for turning you down when you take.

'Huh? How am I going to do that? What if I am a newbie engineer in a group of CEOs?'
Give value.

'How? I don't have anything.'
 Yes, you do. You have your primal resources.
'Can you elaborate?'
Sure.

When you are below status in terms of money, resources & position to a CEO, then it's time to give them what they truly **desire**.

Their true desire is to *feel important.*

You do that by:
1. Listening to them.
2. Asking them questions.
3. Giving genuine compliments.
4. Laughing when they said something funny.

These 4 actions appeal to their primal side.

Higher ups don't care if you give them money. Why do you think they wanted to be higher ups in the first place?

It was so they could be made to **feel important.**

'But doesn't that mean I am ass kissing?'
No.

'How so?'
Because you are doing it with compassion, not with the desire
to get ahead.

Heck, you are going to be acting this way with the janitor, the
interns, the lady serving you soda etc. By making this a
lifestyle & not an act, the mindset flips.

There is no more persona that is required. Instead, it's a game
of genuinely providing value by appealing to someone's
primal desires.

When you do that for long enough, you often don't even have
to ask for anything. THEY will offer. They will wonder how
they can help you.

At that point, since so much time has been invested in the
rapport building phase, a social bond has appeared out of
nowhere.

Once you leave the interaction, they are going to be amazed
by how you said so little but impacted them so much.

A person stops being awkward when they stop being
desperate. They stop being desperate when they stop trying to
take before they give.

Breaking Out Of Shyness

'Come on Arman, just say hello son, you can do it. Come on now' my mom said.
She was starting to get frustrated.
'Just tell your teacher hello.'

But I couldn't do it. I was frozen.
The thoughts were flying & the emotions were starting to get out of control. Is this really happening?

'Wait what's going on bro? Why didn't you want to tell your teacher hello for?'
Because I was terrified.

'Of?'
Of being unleashed into kindergarten by myself.
'Why? What's the big deal?'
My sudden move to the United States had left me in a state of culture shock. Something very bad was happening.
'What?'
I was losing my voice.

The Troublemaking Village kid

Flashback to eight months before

The year was 1997.
I was a 5-year-old living in the village of Bangladesh with my family. We lived in a low-income sector of Bangladesh, with huge farmland & low electronics etc.

At this point in my life, everything felt like a blast.

'Why? You lived in a muddy ass 3rd world country with little to no electricity. Why the hell were you having so much fun?'

Because I felt free, my friend. Our village was a very tight-knit community where we resided right by our grandparents, uncles, aunties, cousins etc. Everyone was so nearby that we could swing by their crib anytime we felt bored.

'How were you like growing up?'
I was a very troublesome talkative kid.
'Oh yea? Got any funny stories about that?'
Ha yea.

In my village, our teachers were much different than the teachers in the US.
'How?'
Whenever we acted out, they would hit us.
'They would put hands on you?'
No. Of course not! They would hit us with rulers.

Let's just say that I was always getting hit with a ruler for talking in class.
'Was that the troublesome part?'
Not quite.

Once I had gotten so mad at the teacher for hitting me that I wanted to get revenge on him. He was this fat, stocky, little man who thought he was all that. Time to put him in his place!

'And how did you do that?'

Well, my teacher and my dad were friends.
He once came over to deliver a package to my dad.

Long story short, I was on the second story of the building &
my teacher was reaching the package upwards for me to
grab it.
'Okay so what the big deal about that?'
Well, I didn't grab the package. Instead, I took out my willy
and began peeing on him!

The bum had no clue I was peeing on him, thought I was
sprinkling water or something. When he found out that the
water was very warm and smelled like piss, he got angry as
hell!

'I'll see you in school Armani!' said my teacher in pure anger.

Although I knew I was going to get an ass beating, getting
the revenge was too sweet to pass up.

Life was good. The life of a village boy was such a unique
experience that I wouldn't trade for the world. I loved
Bangladesh and all the positive vibes that came with it.

Village boy no more

Back to the Present

8 months had passed since I was in my village & now, I was
living in Florida.

The sudden move had been a major culture shock for my

parents, my brother & me.
'Why? What was the big difference?'
Tons.

America used inches, we used centimeters.
America used had Gameboys, we had slingshots.
America had cars, while we had a thing called rickshaws.

But there was one thing that was very difficult to adjust to.
'What was that?'
The language.

Learning the language was no easy task.
But my brother & I were on a time crunch. We had to learn
the language quick!

'Why?'
Because we moved to the country right when the school
semester was about to start.

The time crunch put a lot of pressure on my brother & me.
We had to learn all these words, sentence structures &
grammar.
Writing it was not too difficult, but speaking the language felt
like tackling a whole new beast!

No time to whine.
Tick tock. We need to find a way to figure all this out.

Have 3 weeks to prepare!
Let's get it.

First day of School

3 weeks flew by so quick.
We were pulling up into the school in our minivan.

My mom looked at me. 'Armani, you are going to do well,
okay? Do not be too hard on yourself. You have been
practicing your English a lot for these past few weeks.'

*I don't know mom, I am really nervous. I'll be honest with
you, I don't know if I'm ready to go to school just yet. Can you
just give me one more year to learn the language?*

'No Armani, come on now. Don't give up on me.'
Seriously, just give me one more year.
'No Armani, this is final. Get out of the car.'

We were weaving through the hallways trying to find the
correct classroom. My heartbeat was rising. After a few, my
mom had finally found the class.

There was a woman that was standing outside the classroom
greeting all the new students. Oh boy, time to walk on over.

'Why hello there! What is your name?' said the teacher.
I looked up at her in utter fear.
silence
'All good young man?' said the teacher after a few seconds of
silence.
'Tell your teacher hi Arman' my mom said.

I looked at my teacher frozen.

'Come on Arman. Just say hello son, you can do it. Come on
now.'
My mom gave me a little pinch on the back to tell me to wake

up.
'Just tell your teacher hello.'
But I couldn't.

I was frozen.

I had been studying English so much for the past 3 weeks
that I was trying to pick the perfect words. But the more I was
trying to choose the perfect words, the more the anxiety
built.

The overthinking was causing me to freeze. You could tell my
mom was becoming a little frustrated & upset by my inability
to even introduce myself.

It got so bad that my mom ended up introducing me.
However, my teacher was completely understanding.

'All good! The kids are always nervous on their first day.
Anyways Armani, come with me and let me get you all
situated' said the teacher.

She gently put her palm on my shoulder and began guiding
me into the classroom.

Day 1 in Class

I entered class & there were around 20 other kids already
sitting down. With all the chatter going on, it seemed like the
kids already began forming some friendships.

Me?
I immediately found an empty seat & avoided eye contact

with everyone.

'Were you going to introduce yourself to anyone?'
Hell no! I'm just going to mind my own business. Maybe I will
not have to speak English after all!

The hours flew by, and recess began.

'Hey kid, what is your name?'
I turn around & saw 6 kids staring at me. The kid who asked
me the question was a fat pudgy kid who seemed to be the
leader of the group.

Shit! I made it a few hours without saying anything, what do
I do?
'Hey kid I am talking to you, what is your name?'

Damn. Okay Armani, you have to say something.
'Can you talk bro?' said a few of the other kids from the
group.
Okay fuck it! It's time.

Uh..Meh naiyam ez Arman, I said in pure struggle.

All the kids looked at me, looked at each other & then paused.
'Whatt??? Haha bro, is that how you sound?? Haha.' said the
leader of the group.

Just like that, everyone soon began to join the leader in his
mockery of my accent.
Soon enough, the group was calling in other people from the
class asking me to speak more so they could go ahead and
clown me.

Damn that moment was terrifying. It was the worst-case scenario that was playing out in real life.

This felt like a nightmare.

10 years later

At this point, I was age 15 and in the 10th grade.
'Nice man! How was life treating you since that moment?'
It was different.

'How was it different?'
Remember how I was mentioning that I was this free spirit growing up in the village?

'Yea, so what?'
Well ever since that playground incident, something in me had changed.

'And what was that?'
I was no longer that talkative trouble making kid. I had now transformed into this shy timid kid.

'Wait, all from that playground moment?'
Yea. No clue what happened. But a mix of moving to a brand-new country, having a heavy accent and very little friends had plummeted my confidence.

I was now living the life of a shy kid.
'How was it?'
Awful.

The Impact of Words

6 words that turned me even shyer: *Hey, why are you so quiet?*
Well, it wasn't so much the words.
It was the amount of truth behind the words.

Why am I so damn quiet?
I fucking hate this shit! It's annoying because everyone who knew me really well thought I was the funniest kid they knew.

You know how in Hollywood movies they make that shy kid seem like that sweet, easy going, teddy bear?
Let me tell you something.

That is a **complete** lie.
The life of a shy kid is dark, hard & often times crippling.

I went years being shy. It had become such a big part of my lifestyle that I did not even know that I was shy at this point.

The problem was that there were way too many issues.
Because when you are shy, you are immediately unconfident.

That may not be the politically correct thing to say, but oh well.

The life of a shy fly on the wall was becoming brutal. People often acted like I wasn't even there in a group event.

I remember one very embarrassing moment during class when I raised my hand to answer a question. The teacher blurts out 'Armani is that you raising your hand? You know how to talk?'

And the whole class began to laugh at my expense.

I finished up my high school career being the guy that was virtually known by very few.

The Shyness Spillover

The shy person is too nice & does not create feelings in others. In the social dynamic's world, you know what we call someone who cannot incite feelings in others?
'What?'
Boring.

Being boring will tarnishes likeability, life opportunities & your social life.

Some people are shy because they do not like talking too much, I get it. However, many are shy because they feel too many nerves when they have to talk. The latter described me.

The one hidden gem of being shy

Being shy lowkey gave me one social intelligence superpower.
'And what was that?'
Observation skills.

Observation skills are one of the key components of being socially dynamic.

I had spent YEARS sitting on the sidelines observing so many social interactions that I had learned tons of social dynamics in the process.

At this point, even though I wasn't participating in the conversations, I was able to see many social moves happening even before it happened.

Most shy people notice EVERYTHING.

I had all the knowledge in the world. I just needed to show a little more courage, that's it.

Just a little bit more courage to speak up.
Come on Armani, think of something.

How are you ever going to make something of yourself if you can't speak up? You have all the ideas in the world, but how you will you ever be known?
Something has to change.

Destiny

I looked up tons of articles on how to stop being shy. But I kept seeing the generic 'talk to more people' articles.

'Well, why didn't you talk to more people?'
It's because I was too nervous & wanted to find a shortcut.

I wanted to cheat code out of shyness.
'How were you going to do that?'
By conquering something that terrifies many. If I conquer this fear, then there is no way I am still shy.

'And what is that?'
Public Speaking.

Toastmaster

I invested the next few months into Toastmasters.
It was **brutal**.

For my first ever speech, I choked so bad that I ran away like
a little bitch for months.

I ended up being beating myself up for being such a wimp.
My confidence had plummeted so low after my choke job that
I wanted to quit altogether.

Still, quitting was simply not something that was an option.
Despite taking months off from entering a Toastmasters
event, I knew that I had to go back.

As the famous saying goes, 'You can take a break, but you
must never quit.'

After **months & months** of being a bonafide bum, I finally
had the courage to step back into the battlefield. Time to re-
enter the Toastmasters world.

The choke job + the months of shame had me feeling so bad,
that nothing could top that. Strangely, I felt more confident
because I had this, 'I've already embarrassed myself enough,
what can beat that' mentality.

Very odd way to build confidence, but it *worked.*

Speech after speech

I joined 3 Toastmasters clubs so I could go full force Super
Saiyan mode into the public speaking world.

Speech, get evaluated, get feedback, apply to next speech.

That was the lifecycle for the next few months. Each speech
taught me more about myself. Each talk felt like a workout
for my internal world & for my low tier confidence.

Getting on stage so much soon had me viewing my nerves of
anxiety as an adrenaline rush. My fear of public speaking
began to melt after I kept it going with the speeches.

'Good job. But what does this have to do with your shyness?'
Public speaking changed my mentality.

Can fixing speech anxiety cure social anxiety?

From my experience? Yes.
Fixing speech anxiety fixed my social anxiety & my shyness
melted from the process.

My initial theory of conquering the number 1 fear on the
planet tested out to be true!

Working on my public speaking had helped
out **tremendously** with my social interactions. It was
amazing to witness.

'Wait, how did public speaking help you talk to people?'
Because think about it!

You are maintaining a fluid tonality, eye contact, utilizing confident body language in front of tons of people. You're telling me that 1 on 1 conversations will not feel easier after all that?

Plus, conquering public speaking also does one more thing. It took me a level above shyness.

It legit makes you confident, not just some person who is existing. Mainly because of overcoming the #1 fear in the world.

Who will not feel confident after that?

Where do you go from here?

There are 2 basic frameworks to get started to conquer shyness.

Path 1: Toastmasters.

This is the method that I used to overcome shyness. Join a club & make the effort to give as many speeches as you can. It is a very safe community so don't be too hard on yourself for messing up.

Path 2: Participate in more social events.

If you do not have too many friends, then I recommend

starting off with 'Meetup' events. You get to go to different club events that handle different niches. *Wine tasting, cryptocurrency, paddle boating etc.*

For path 2 strategy, you are doing more 1 on 1 interactions vs path 1 where you are talking to a crowd.

Path 2 may take a little bit longer, but it will get you on the right track! All you have to do is keep moving forward every day.

Choose Your Path!

Few things to look out for in your social interactions...

So at this point, I hope you have been utilizing the positives of your shyness, which are your *observation skills.*

You should be a good listener already.
If that is the case, then you are **very** close to charisma.

You just need to talk ~30% of the conversation. Anything less than that will give you the shy label.
My personal charisma formula is:
30 % speaking & 70 % listening.

Play around with your numbers as you begin your journey to overcoming your shyness.

Now get to work.

Reputation

Seinfeld was one of the most popular shows to ever have been released. It was a show about nothing. Which made the concept even more entertaining!

Ironically, the character who stood out the most to me wasn't Seinfeld.

It was Kramer.
The eccentric, neighbor who was always up to something.

Kramer was a lot of people's favorite character. Without him, the show would not have been the same.

After Seinfeld had ended, all the cast members were now off to their own path. As was Michael Richards, the actor who played Kramer.

Around 2006, there was footage from the Laugh Factory released of Michael Richards responding to a heckler and it wasn't pretty.

He went on a racist tirade dropping the N word at a few African Americans.
Chaos ensued.

Just like that, Michael Richards reputation was tarnished.

Years of hard work was wiped out like a sandcastle that was made too close to the waves. There was no rewind button.

Michael played a huge role in his reputation being soiled. He was the one who allowed rage to get the best of him. The most he was able to do was apologize afterwards & show genuine remorse.

What do you do when you aren't playing a huge role in having your reputation being damaged? What if someone is spreading lies about you?

I see it all the time. There can be a breakup for example.

All the ex does is bad mouth their former partner. While in reality, it was the ex who was the toxic one. Sad, but it happens.

Or when you do something honestly and a hater comes out the woodwork trying to undermine your success.

This may not be fair, but it happens in the social world.

Which is why it is important to focus on character over reputation.

Other people who believe the hater or an ex talking sideways without hearing your side of the story weren't real anyways. They would have switched up on you the first chance they got. These aren't people you want to be associating with.

Character, you can always control.
Reputation, you can't always control.

Sometimes, you'll have a strong say in your reputation. Other times, you'll be helpless.

Focus on character & you'll build the right reputation with the right people. Not everyone will every like you. Opinions change like the wind.

Rage is not pretty & the effects can follow you for a long time.
Catch the signs before it happens & compose or exit the
scenario.

Easier said than done, I know.

Bouncing Back from Tough Times

Normally, I do my best to get a haircut once a month. Preferably, the first week of every month. But this all depends on my barber's schedule.

I've had a lot of barbers in my life. Most of them ended up messing up my hair. However, my newest barber knows my hairstyle well.

His name is Joey. A guy who is a few years older than me & pretty laid back.

When I go to get my hair cut, we talk about business, life, some random stuff & I dip. The social bond is not more complicated than that.

Well, on one particular month, I go to get my haircut & notice that Joey was very quiet. Wasn't saying much. Even if I asked him a question, he was short.

A tad bit awkward, but it's okay. I was in the mood to just chill myself.

As the haircut is wrapping up, he says:

'My bad bro. I'm a little out of it. My girl just dumped me recently & I'm feeling sad.'

There was a weird vibe in the air & now it made sense. I asked him what he was going to do next.

He said that he was just going to do his own thing & try to level up. But still sounded shaky.

As he was edging me up, he kept talking about their memories. The good old days. And how he feels very sad.

Around that time, I decided to recommend the book, The Power of Now by Eckhart Tolle.

The basic gist of the book is to live in the present moment. That's all we ever have. It's a great book for anyone who is going through rock bottom.

My barber made a note of it in his phone. I was not sure if he actually wrote anything down.

The haircut wrapped up. I wished him the best & left.

Recently, when I got my haircut with him again, he seemed like a different person.
'Yo bro, I have been reading that Power of Now book. That dude Eckhart is a G' he said.

I was surprised that he read the book. A lot of people don't read nowadays. But rock-bottom can bring out your best side or your worst side.

He seemed more chill this time. I asked him how he was dealing with the breakup.

He said he was doing well. He had been working on his barbershop business, getting more clients & learning real estate on the side.

This was a good situation to hear.

Breakups can often derail people for many years.

I knew a poised individual in college who could never get over his ex. Went from being poised to becoming an alcoholic & slowly tarnishing his friend circle with a lot of antics.

It's tough to go through a difficult time in today's world. Everyone seems to be busy & dealing with problems themselves.

The information age atomized a big part of society which causes for a lot of pressure on each individual body.

Which is why emotional intelligence is a skillset that pays dividends to your sanity.

A way to bounce back from tough times is via information. If you have people skills & are well read, then recommending the right book to the right person at the right time is a game changer.

It's because information can give perspective. Perspective enhances perception. And perception is the reason you are in rock bottom in the first place.

Things aren't bad.
Things are neutral.

However, our thinking is what assigns a subjective experience to a neutral act, coloring the event.

After reading the Power of Now, my barber was like:

'Damn man, I thought I had it bad due to a breakup. But Eckhart was thinking about committing suicide. My problem wasn't THAT bad.'

That perspective helps a ton. Informing yourself allows you to pull yourself out of rock bottom with your own helping hand.

That's how you build confidence for the future.

Others will help in the process too, don't get me wrong. But that may not always be the case for everyone. Some people don't have any friends.

'Don't have any friends? Yea right bro!'
 Yep, that happens at times.

People who go through rock bottom don't have any friends. They may have acquaintances, but no close ties like that.

That's why I recommend investing in a core squad of at least 2-5 people. That beats having way too many friends because during rock bottom, those 2-5 stay around.

The others get busy or switch sides on you. Seen it happen many times.

The main insight in bouncing back from tough times is knowing that you can.

There's not only one rock-bottom in life. That is an illusion. There are many.

However, the problems that would take you out for months don't even take you out for a few days as you begin to get tougher.

The main thing about getting tougher is having a set of personalized moments of knowing when you were tough.

Even if the event took you out for some time, you were eventually able to bounce back.

That's the beauty of tough moments because ultimately no one can fight the battles fully for you. Especially the rewiring the perception's part.

That's on you bud.

Know that you can overcome tough moments by recalling all the moments in the past when you have done it. If you can't recall any moments in the past, then make this rock-bottom moment the memory for your future.

Random stuff happens. Throughout that, be the anchor in your own life.

People can come and go. But the person across the mirror will always remain the same.

Why Authenticity is Harder than It Looks

In 2013, there was this radio personality named Charlamagne tha God who was blowing up in the hip hop space.

He was a radio personality for the show, Breakfast Club.

There was a targeted audience who resonated with him because he asked tough questions to musicians & often made inappropriate comments.

One of his most famous moments was making the rapper Lil Mama cry on air.

What I noticed was that people dubbed Charlamagne as 'authentic.' If you were to ask me, he just seemed like an asshole.

However, his numbers did not lie. He was a big factor in making the Breakfast Club one of the most popular radio shows.

As 7 years passed, Charlamagne seems like a different guy. He seems like he matured a bit.

In one of his recent interviews, he was trying to give some advice to an upcoming artist who was spreading a bunch of negative energy.

And that younger artist scoffed at him & was like:
'Man, I know you aren't talking. You are the king of negative energy!'

Charlamagne looked pretty taken aback and asked:
'What, people can't grow?'

Charlamagne had a point. However, his negative energy was coming back to haunt him.

Question is, which Charlamagne was the real one? The one back then or the one now?

Better question is, what is authenticity?

It's difficult to be authentic due to 2 important variables:

1. Life is constantly throwing us different experiences requiring a different version of ourselves.
2. Authenticity requires reflection.

The first point can be seen in our present moment. An example is when you have to wear different hats in a social interaction.

Like when you are talking to a shy kid vs a talkative kid. If you are capable of adjusting, each person will see a different version of you.

The shy kid will see the talkative side to you.
The talkative kid will see the listening side to you.

You're the same person.

Yet, your behavior changed.

Another reason authenticity is difficult is because it requires reflection. Reflection also requires 2 important variables:
-The ability to control thinking.
-Humility.

Some people can't focus for more than 10 seconds. So, reflecting becomes tougher. That's where a journal can help. It forcefully slows down your thoughts.

Cool, a journal can help slow down your thoughts.
But what about the humility part?

Well, that's something we are on our **own** with.
No assistance.

I've known 2 brothers for over 10 years.

The younger brother seems light years ahead of the older brother in terms of maturity. The older brother seems like a bigger jackass year by year.

The dude is aging.
However, he isn't growing up.
Why?

It's because humility can't be bought. It's a game of going in & learning the difference between cocky & confident on a FIRSTHAND basis.

Overall, authenticity is a game of refining.

It's a game of doing our best to realize who we truly are.

Since starting the ArmaniTalks, I've talked about social skills, public speaking & human dynamics from MANY different angles.

Each time, I came to realize that the communication with the outside world is mainly based off the communication with the inside world.

The 5 levels of communication are:

1. Communication with self = **Self awareness**
2. Communication with 1 person = **Dialogue**
3. Many to Many communication = **Group Interaction**
4. One to many communication = **Public Speaking**
5. Communication + Technology = **Media**

1 is the most important.
1 influences 2 - 5.

However, most of us view it as the exact opposite. We focus on 2-5 hoping to figure out 1.

This method can work, sure. But it will be suboptimal at best.

The world of communication...
The game of the outside world.....
Has a strange way of consistently directing us to the inside world.

Great communicators with depth focus predominantly on building their self-awareness.

By asking what stage they currently reside in and how can humility be assessed?

Authenticity has many layers.

For others to know the real version of you, you have to put in the leg work & find out the real version...*for yourself.*

Conor McGregor

Conor McGregor has been a very interesting fellow for the past couple of years, a great resource to learn soft skills from.

'Soft skills? Isn't he a fighter?'
Yes.

I believe learning soft skills from a fighter further amplifies the tangible aspects of soft skills.

Fighting in itself is not the high value product.
The CONTENT of fighting is what made UFC a force to be reckoned with in the sports world.

What I mean by that is that a skilled fighter is great.
However, a skilled fighter simply fighting in a geographic location takes away the leverage.

Combine the skilled fighter with pay per-view, content, a miniseries etc. and now we have a **product**.

The reason I said this is because Conor McGregor has 2 soft skills that allowed him to scale. It was visualization & public speaking.

He was a skilled trash talker. That allowed casual fans to take interest in fighting.

Also, in his words, he mentioned how much he would visualize his success leading up to his meteoric rise.

He wasn't a guy who just visualized and called it a day.
Rather, he used visualization as a force multiplier alongside an insane work ethic.

Those 2 soft skills are what made him a star.
Not just the fighting skills alone.

However, it feels as though his rise fizzled out.
Where has he been?

At the time of writing this, Conor has a much-anticipated fight with Dustin Porier coming up.
Which is good news. But once again, what about the meteoric rise from a couple of years ago?

The sad truth is that he was involved in a lot of setbacks. To getting in bar fights, throwing a chair at a bus, getting caught smashing a fan's phone etc.

You could argue that he is a cautionary tale of what it meant to be a loser.
Not a winner.

However, I recently watched one of Conor's interviews and he seems like a different person, with a blend of the same attitude.

He seems different, as in not talking as much trash. He is a father now & seems much more mature. That part is different.

What's the same is his surreal confidence.

For a guy who had only one fight in 2020 and hasn't been highly active...He still has supreme confidence in his skillset.

This is often what we don't see about top performers.

Their comeback.

I'm not saying that Conor is going to win his fight with
Dustin. But from his tone, HE believes he is going to win his
fight tonight.
That's called having faith in yourself.

We often talk about confidence.
What is confidence?
Can it be defined?

One definition is 'feeling whole.'

Good definition.
Seems general.
Can we get more specific?

Well, let's break it down in a series.
Confidence = Faith in yourself.
Faith = Intense belief.
Belief = When mind aligns with body & body aligns with
mind.

This loop is what creates confidence.

'When body aligns with mind & mind aligns with body?
Huh??'
That's something we need to understand.

You ever got in really good shape?
Took a break...then came back?

When you came back, there was muscle memory. You were able to pick up the moves much faster this time.
That's the memory of the body.

Likewise, there is a mind memory as well.
Plus, there is a mind-body memory as well.

I said earlier that Conor always visualized his success. He paired it up with insane work ethic.
Well nowadays, he has confidence in himself more so in a realm of muscle memory.

In a logical world, for him to believe in himself despite being so inactive seems ridiculous.
However, the world of confidence does not always have to be logical.

All this goes to show that soft skills leaves its trails behind greatness.

Because to become great, one eventually needs to win over the mind.

How one wins over the mind is up to them.
But greatness requires an understanding of the mental faculties to command the mental faculties.

Will Conor win?
No clue.

However, it's hard to hate on the attitude of someone with intense self-belief.

Social Unintelligence: The Subtle Diss

In the 5th grade, I used to sit in lunch with this kid named CJ.

CJ and I were good friends & always had good conversations during lunch time. Both of us were quiet, so we didn't have this HUGE circle that we rolled with.

As the school year progressed, I noticed CJ becoming friends with this kid named Joseph Danahoo.

I didn't like Joseph.

Not because CJ was becoming friends with him, but because Joseph was too sarcastic for my liking. For some strange reason, CJ couldn't get enough of the guy.

One day, CJ & I were having lunch, and we both saw Joseph pull up to a nearby table. He was by himself.

'Hey Armani, I will be right back. I need to tell Joe something,' said CJ.

Alright, cool bro.

What's weird was CJ took his lunch tray with him & sat down with Joe.

They began chatting & laughing away.
The minutes began to pile on.

Needless to say, CJ never came back. He left me sitting alone in the table that day. He subtly dissed me.

I was pretty angry at CJ to be honest. For the rest of the year, I decided not to talk to him. There were times he tried to sit with me or hang out with me after class, but I wasn't having it.

I went onto make new friends. CJ had no clue what happened between us.

He had no clue.

Looking back, I knew I shouldn't have had been so passive aggressive. I should have spoken to him, man to man.

Well, we were in 5th grade at the time, so mini man to mini man.

If that was the case, then who knows, the friendship could have been salvaged.

I have no clue what CJ is up to nowadays. Where he lives. Or if him or Joseph are even friends anymore.

I share this story because the social world is very nuanced.

Be honest. Have you ever done something like what CJ did?

Say you're hanging out with a coworker & you bump into an old friend. You begin chatting it up with the old friend & completely ignore the person you were initially hanging out with.

Or let's say you are at a party, and you are taking to this person. Out of nowhere, they excuse them self & begin talking to someone else. They left you hanging.

It's stuff like this you want to be aware of.

In CJ's case, I wouldn't have taken it personally if he did so much as to invite me to sit with him. It's all a game of social intelligence.

The MEGA key to communication skills is treating others like they are the main character of their world.

If you can do that to success, then you will have a:
- o   Powerful social network.
- o   Powerful personal brand.
- o   A powerful business.

The world is a game of people. Those who can play the game will rise.

There's no worse feeling than losing a game that you never had a clue that you were playing.

Why Nice Guys Finish Last

Being nice & being kind are different.

-A nice guy = real or fake with a polite delivery.
-A kind guy = real with a polite delivery.

The nice guy chases **approval**.
The kind guy chases **authenticity**.

My Toastmasters club had this nice guy in it a couple of years back.

His name was Tom. Great person don't get me wrong. But he would always be so fidgety & giggly. It made everyone uncomfortable.

He had been in Toastmasters for a few years. So nowadays, he was the guy mainly evaluating speeches.

The evaluator has one of the most important roles in Toastmasters. A solid evaluation brings awareness to certain holes in a speech for new or veteran speakers. And that awareness pays dividends for the speaker down the line.

Well, with Tom being so nice, he would never say anything remotely critical. He'd just talk about what the speaker did right. Even when there were times when the speaker did many things wrong.

An evaluation is not supposed to be a flurry of criticism.

Rather, it's supposed to be:
**What they did right + What they could improve +
Reinforce what they did right.**

What they did right represents the buns. What they could
improve represents the patty. That's the evaluation sandwich.

Tom was just giving out the buns. But he never had the guts
to deliver the patty.

This probably seemed noble in the eyes of Tom. However, it
had the other Toastmasters members having to finish the job
afterwards.

They were now put in a predicament to point out what the
speaker should improve so they could level up.

There was one new speaker who had his back turned to half
of the audience the WHOLE time.

Tom thought it would be mean to point it out.

 In the end, Tom finished last in the race. Nice guys always
finish last for that reason. The nice guy lacks **intention**.

When someone lacks intention, they have no clue if you they
are winning or losing.

'How do people get over the nice guy syndrome?'
2 ways.

   o   Through a sudden traumatizing moment.

Or

   o   Through consistency.

For the first path, you don't have much say in the matter. Let's say you get fired from a job that you have been in for 15 years. No backup plans or anything. Well, that's a shock that will hopefully teach you about human nature.

For path 2, you can begin today.
Be consistent in investing in yourself.
Do something worth feeling proud of.

So, when you enter an interaction, you aren't automatically placing yourself as the lower social valued individual.

The title of this talk is that nice guys finish last, but truth be told, they often don't even enter the race.

The social world doesn't reward nice. It rewards real. That's why the kind guy is always laps ahead.

Reading the Same Book Multiple Times

There are readers who read the same book multiple times. On repeat.

But why?
If you read it once, why read it again??

I would ponder this question as I watched reruns of Everybody Loves Raymond. Used to watch that show so much that I had plenty of the lines memorized.

But younger me didn't catch the irony of watching the same sitcom over and over again. Then questioning why people read the same book over and over again.

'Why did you keep on watching Everybody Loves Raymond?'
Because it was my favorite show.

Each time I watched it, I found something in the show that I hadn't noticed before. Sometimes, I noticed something big & other times, it was tiny.

As I got older, I started to realize the same concept held true with reading. Each time you read, you read from a new lens.

Finding the right book is all about quality. There are plenty of books that I can re-read over and over again. However, I don't find the need.

'How do you know which one was right to re-read?'

I wish I could give you a logical response but I can't.

It was a FEELING.

As I read the book, I saw myself in it. Each word resonated with me. Felt like it was designed for me.

When a book is right for you, your entire nervous system gets engaged. The body feel lighter, a few tingles in the spine, and a strong sensation in the chest.

It's not something that I only noticed. Talked to plenty of people who have reported back on the same sensations. So, stay alert for these sensations.

Re-reading a book multiple times turns words into pictures and pictures into principles.

No matter which book is out there, reread it **if you see yourself in it.**

It doesn't just speak to the head.
It speaks to the heart.

Each time you re-read a book, you go from surface level to depth level. No longer the waves. But it's a matter of experiencing how deep the ocean goes.

Awareness expands.

Maybe I should bring this up.
No copying.

Just because a book resonates with someone else's life doesn't mean it will necessarily resonate with yours.

Each time you read a page; it feels different.
Each time you read a chapter; it feels different.
Each time you read the book; it feels different.

The words are the same. But the person reading it, is different.

The XFL

You remember watching the World Wrestling Federation (WWF) back in the days?

'Yes. Triple H, The Rock, Stone Cold. Those were the days.'
It sure was.

My brother and I used to stay up late to watch the WWF. We loved the story lines. If you missed an episode, then you were behind in the conversations at school the next day in class.

Vince McMahon was the CEO of the WWF. During the late 90s & early 2000s, he was seen as a marketing genius. A wizard when it came to entertainment on television.

He was so hyped about being a marketing genius, that he decided to expand his portfolio. He decided he was going to try his hand at football.

NFL watch out.
XFL is on the horizon.

'How did he do?'
Truth be told, it may have been too soon to tell.

Within a year, the ratings were not what he hoped and the media pounced on Vince.

This guy was supposed to be a marketing genius. *How come the ratings aren't higher??* the media wondered.

The media did not like Vince too much. They were waiting for him to fail.

'Why didn't the media like him?'
Because they felt that the WWF was cheap entertainment and was responsible for a lot of the violence in society.

But then again, they may have been just looking for a story.

There came a day when Vince McMahon went on Bob Costas's show to answer some questions about the XFL. What was supposed to be a respectable dialogue turned into a heated interview.

In summary, Bob was clowning Vince for the poor ratings. Vince was saying that he needed more time to build a brand. Bob asked what he will do if the ratings did not rise up?

Vince said he will continue fighting.

That's the main thing I got from the interview. The fighter's mindset part.

A few months later, the XFL was dropped and shut down and it was a humiliating defeat for Vince McMahon. He finally had a big black hole in his entrepreneurship career.

Years went on by...

One day, I was coming back to my apartment & noticed my neighbors getting super lit. One of them came outside & asked:

'You aren't watching the game??'
Game? What game? I asked.
'The XFL game.'

What?? Over a decade later, and the XFL is back??

I thought my neighbor was joking.
But no.

The league had returned.
Rose up like the Phoenix from the ashes.

I normally don't watch too much TV, so I had no clue this was the case. But thought it was dope. A blast from the past.

What made it more dope was how much positive reception it was getting on social media. A lot of people were having fun watching this league.

It showed that Vince was right:
He is a fighter.

How successful will the XFL be?
I have no clue and that's not the point.

The point of this story is to keep on fighting. Doesn't matter what you are working on, just keep the momentum going.

There will be times where you are backed into a corner, and you may be forced into taking a break. Sort of like Vince was when his channel dropped him.

But he had the vision to realize that he will just push the project aside. Until he brings it back...
YEARS later.

There are certain times to have the awareness to pick up when something is a dead horse.

But there are other times when you need to just keep it pushing.

The XFL fell into the latter boat. I'm hoping for its success.

Just goes on to show that perseverance will take you far.

'How far?'
Only the future will tell.

Who knows, you may have a project like the XFL up your sleeve.

Dangers of Small Thinking

Communication skills at the core is an exchange of ideas.

What is an idea?
A thought.
What is a thought?
Thinking patterns which create an output.

The beauty of Twitter is that you get to see how your thinking works. Along with that, you get to see how other people's thinking works as well.

There was a tweet I wrote a couple of months back talking about mindset.

Then someone with the word 'meditation' in her Twitter handle commented something. The comment was agreeing with my initial tweet. I thought everything was done.

But no, everything was not done.

Right after, there was a guy who commented about her handle. He wrote 'just wanted you to know, meditation is imitation prayer.'
Something like that.

From there, those 2 began debating.

What this gentleman showed was **small thinking.** He was

creating controversy in his own mind because he was comparing 2 things which didn't need comparison.

"I like my right hand more! My left hand is just an imitation of my right hand. Fuck that!"
That's all I heard when he made that ridiculous comment.

Meditation can be used for spiritual reasons. But it can also be used to control the mind for better practical benefits in life. No one willingly turns down the ability to concentrate better.

Turn the mind into matter and then the matter can be controlled by the senses. That's the essence of meditation.

If you break it down, meditation can help someone become BETTER at praying.

Who wants to pray while thinking about 10 different things?
crickets
The danger of small thinking fools the mind into thinking that it's a winner stamping its authority. While the small thoughts just make the person look like an idiot.

I know, because I used to be one of those guys.
A dualistic thinker.
A right or wrong thinker.

Dualistic thinking can work great while making decisions. Gives a framework for how to behave.

However, applying dualistic thinking on other humans is where chaos ensues.
'Why?'
Due to ideals.

All humans do not have the same ideals. What Jerimiah
wants from his life may be COMPLETELY different from what
Raiana wants.

If Jerimiah is using his ideals to measure Raiana as a person,
then he is losing the race from the very beginning. He is
going to have a terribly busy, low ROI life.

**A big thing about maturing is learning how NOT to have
an opinion on something.**
Learning that your ideals don't match another person's ideals.
And that's okay.

That's a key to clear communication.

- o *Small thinking happens when you think you know it
  all.*
- o *Ironically, big thinking happens when you accept you
  don't know it all.*

It doesn't feel intuitive to the ego, but that's just how the game
works.

Small thinkers destruct more than they build. The tough part
is that we are all small thinkers in certain fields.

Knowledge dissipates the ignorance.

This is exactly why lifelong learning and communication
skills go hand in hand. The more the mind stretches, the
smoother one becomes with words.

The Spotlight Effect

Ever had the *feeling* like you were being watched?

You were super nervous to go into the networking event because you *felt* like all eyes were going to be on you.

And now that you are in the event, all the smiling *faces* looks like they are hiding their **real** intentions.

You think they are thinking about you.
Judging you.

This leads to uncomfortable body language. And worse...Friends are confused as enemies.

The ironic thing?
Other people are doing the **same** thing.

This phenomenon is known as: *'Spotlight Effect.'*

The Spotlight Effect is a psychological illusion that makes a person believe there is a figurative spotlight on their head. Causing others to overanalyze them.

This typically occurs in social events.

The question is why?
It's because of the human ego.

The human ego makes us view ourselves as the main character of our story. This leads us to enter different venues thinking that we are serving as the main character of the event.

But the reality is that other people feel the same way. They are the main character of their stories as well. You are nothing more than an extra in their world.

To seal this concept further, understand this.
Your WORST problem will not be registered as more important than their most MINUSCULE problem.

Example:

Say you totaled your car & you tell Billy about it. Billy will feel sympathy and then go back to his everyday life. His mind will refocus from your car to how angry he is at his dog for pooping on the carpet.

Your problem is mainly a problem to you. But for the other person? You are an extra. A peasant. They are the king of their kingdom.
Therefore, they will allocate their mental bandwidth to their issues.

This concept should strangely make you feel **liberated**.

It's one of those concepts when FULLY internalized will melt social anxiety for good.

Yet, the ego hates internalizing this concept.
'What do you mean I am not the main character in someone else's world??' the ego yells.

This is where you begin reconditioning the mind with rationale. The untamed ego cannot even spell rationale. But the tamed ego sure can.

The next time you are about to enter a social event & you feel like all eyes are going to be on you, RECALL THE SPOTLIGHT EFFECT.
Use your rationale.

All the other people are worried about what sort of impression they are going to make. Knowledge adds *fire* to darkness.

Now you are equipped with this knowledge to maneuver around the notion that you're the main character of someone else's life.

This realization will have you feeling bolder & more powerful than ever.

How to Handle a Hater

The lost Internet

One week, I mysteriously lost connection with my internet. I tried everything I could to get it to work.

I rebooted the modem, tried refreshing the connection, logged out & logged back in. But nothing worked.

After an hour of trying & not having any luck, I decided to call the Internet provider.

I ended up spending another hour on call with them trying to get it sorted out.

'Well, did it work?'
Nope.

They had no clue what the problem was. They said that they were going to send a service man to get it all sorted out.

I was a little bummed out, but guess I had no choice but to wait.

The Hulk

The next day, the service man came. He was huge & looked like the hulk! Roughly around his mid-20s, 6 feet, and Hispanic. His name was Ricky.

Ricky told me that he would take a look at the connection with the wires & see what was causing the problem.

After fiddling with a few of the wires, he was immediately able to spot the problem. He said it would take him 20 minutes to get everything sorted out.

After 20 minutes flew by, he knocked on my door & told me that everything was all set. He said that the problem was so small that he wasn't going to charge me for it.

He just had one favor to ask for.
'What?'
Water.

The Conversation

He came inside & I grabbed him a water bottle. From there on, we sparked up a conversation.

Ricky told me that he had been working as an internet provider for the past 4 weeks & was doing bodybuilding on the side. I asked him what he did before all of this.

His response?
He was rapping.

A rapper??? How the hell do you go from being a rapper to an internet technician? Where is the similarity?

So, I began asking him more questions to see how he made the transition. He kept dancing around it at first. But soon enough, he began to open up.

'How come Ricky stopped rapping??'
Ricky stopped rapping because of the criticism.
'Get out of here!'
I'm serious.

Ricky said that him & his friends were producing some fire
music. And as they started creating more music, they started
gaining more attention.

Soon enough, they were performing in clubs, creating music
videos & were gaining exposure on social media.

'Dang, that's amazing!'
But remember...When you generate attention, you can get
good reception. But don't forget, you can also get the bad
reception.

The Two Sides of the Coin

As Ricky's career was beginning to grow in Florida, so did his
haters. He started receiving some boos in crowds & a lot of
negative comments on social media.

He became rattled.

As Ricky was telling me the story about his haters, you could
see his fingers begin to tighten up. He was getting
irritated talking about them.

Yes, it was evident. The haters had gotten under Ricky's skin.

The Dark Side to Growth

Ricky is just one of the many examples of the dark side of growth.

'What is the dark side?'
Haters.

You see, whenever you escape your comfort zone, one thing that comes with it is criticism. This is just a part of human nature.

'Why can't everyone be nice to me?'
Because that's not how the real-world works.

The real-world has a lot of negative people who are just looking to tear someone down. But this shouldn't really bother you.

'Why not? They are hurting my feelings!'
They are hurting your feelings because you don't know the psychology quite yet. Let me give you a little insight into the mind of a hater & how you should go about handling it.

Hater 101

One major thing about haters is that they are always losers.

These people do not have much going on for them. They are the people who spectate & watch from the sidelines.

As a spectator, what happens?
They want to contribute.

Now from here, there are 2 kinds of people.

The critics & haters.

The critics will surprisingly give you a lot of information to help you grow. They will often tell you what you are doing wrong. But they will also tell you how you can improve.

The haters are the ones who simply talk shit & run their mouth. They don't offer any value in return.

'Why do they do this?'
Because you are doing what they wish they could.

So what happens? The feel jealousy! And they use jealousy to build resentment rather than to be inspired.

Therefore, to make themselves bigger & relevant, they attempt to tear others down.

Hater mindset 101.

What You Should Do

When people ask me how they should deal with haters, I always give the same response.

Ignore.

'Why not attack back?'
Because that requires time & energy from your end.
'But isn't it worth it?'
Nope. Let me explain with an analogy.

You see 2 shirts. 1 that you like. 1 that you don't like. And you have enough money to buy both.

What are you buying?
'The one that I like of course!'
Why not buy the one that you don't like as well?
'Because that would be a waste of my money.'
Okay, makes sense.

You see 2 people. 1 is a fan. 1 is a hater.And you have enough time & energy to give to both.

What are you doing?
'Give focus ONLY to the fan? Am I right?'
Correct!

Time & energy are way more valuable than money.

Why waste your time & energy on the wrong person when you feel so stingy spending money on the wrong shirt?

THINK!!

The Power of Ignoring

Now you know why there are haters. You know what to do. Lastly, I want to tell you why ignoring is the strategy of winners.

Ignoring is the strategy of winners because:

1. It exercises your self-control muscle.
2. It gets in the haters head.
3. It allows you to focus on creating.

1. It exercises your self-control muscle.

Whenever you can tame your ego AND emotions to make a

mature decision, you have exercised self-control. Working out this muscle spills over to other parts of your life making self-control much easier in multiple avenues!

2. It gets in the haters head.

Haters don't care if it's good or bad attention. They just like any sort of attention! If you can rob them of that, it rattles them. They wonder how you occupy some much space in their head & they occupy none in yours.

3. It allows you to focus on creating

Don't be a Ricky. Don't let the words of others ever stop you from producing. When you learn the art of ignoring, you can focus FULL energy on creating.

Closing thoughts

The answer is so simple that it seems too easy to be true. But no.

The ignore, refocus & produce tactic will work wonders!

Understand that no matter which field you are in, that you will have to deal with criticism.

Don't let it stop you from moving forward in your path. Because when you are looking back in a few years, you are going to see how silly caring about opinions are in the first place.

All illusions.
Focus on the BIGGER picture.

Now get back out there! Know who to focus your attention on, gather your tribe, & carve out your legacy.

Bingo.

Hypnotize Yourself

Hypnosis.

When you picture the word, you probably see some creepy old man swinging a watch in front of you reciting:

'You are getting verrrryyyy sleepy.'

 Accurate?
'Accurate.'

Point is, we all have our unique interpretation of hypnosis. And unfortunately, most interpretations are highly inaccurate.

On TV, you'll see a hypnotist as someone who is sinister & is playing with human behaviors. But that's not the full picture. Let's break down hypnosis.

In simple terms:
Hypnosis is when the brain is highly susceptible to suggestions.

This typically happens in many ways. One way is through intense focus. Picture the situation of the hypnotist swinging the watch.

It's not the watch that makes a person hypnotized. It's the *intense focus* on the watch that makes the person hypnotized.

Whenever there is a laser like focus on something, a person is put in a trance like state which makes the mind more open to suggestions.

Storytelling is a form of hypnosis. A good storyteller will seamlessly create mental movies which will cause the recipient to be in a trance like state.

But let's go deeper. Let's say you want to hypnotize yourself, what do you do?

Well, it's a matter of walking down memory lane.
'Why memory lane?'
It's because your inner child holds the answers.

Up to the age of ~7 years old, the subconscious mind is like a sponge. A child absorbs everything around them.

That's because the child's brain is operating in Theta waves. Theta waves are when the brain is highly open to suggestions *(more on this shortly)*.

'Why isn't it easy for my brain to absorb suggestions later in life?'
It's because the brain waves *change* as you mature.

The 4 Important Types of Brain Waves for an Adult:
-Beta: Consciousness
-Alpha: Relaxed
-Delta: Sleeping
-Theta: When you are waking up or going to sleep.

As I mentioned, around the age of ~7, your brain is operating in the Theta waves. That is when your brain is most receptive to suggestions!!

Notice something from my Brain Waves list?

As an adult, you are in the Theta state TWO times in the day.
When you are waking up or going to sleep. That is when
your brain is **highly** open for suggestions.

Aka: Hypnosis.

'Wait, really?'
Yes!!

As you are waking up, you are still in a dream like state.
And as you are about to go to sleep, you are about to enter a
dream like state.

That is your opportunity to HYPNOTIZE YOURSELF.

Remember this. Your current reality is a projection of your
subconscious mind.

Your conscious mind can try to make all the changes it
wants, but unless your subconscious mind complies, it will be
tough.

The point of hypnotizing yourself is to you make your
subconscious mind comply.

During those 2 times in the day:

-Visualize your future self. Use your imagination.
-Practice gratitude.
-Consume empowering content.

The average bubba starts their morning & ends their night
with checking their phone.

During these 2 times, they can hypnotize themselves & rewire
their mind, yet they choose to waste it.

Scratch that, I lied.

They do hypnotize themselves. Just towards the wrong direction.

Don't be like them.
Be different.

Quick recap:

1. Hypnosis = Trance like state where the brain is open to suggestions.

2. Hypnosis is best during the Theta brain waves.

3. You have Theta brain waves when you wake up & as you go to sleep.

Two opportunities throughout the day champ.

Use them wisely. Deprogram limiting beliefs & install the empowering beliefs to reboot your life!

The Art of Over Communicating

In 2019, I was working with a client to help her develop an online presence. She used to be a former radio host, so I thought it would be great to help her get started with a podcast.

We can work on the messaging, storytelling & value providing. This was going to be great!

After 1 hour of talking, I thought she would be getting hyped. But certain eye movements told a different story.

Something didn't seem right...

After a while, I asked her if everything was okay. She hesitated for a second. Then responded with:
'You mind if I ask you a stupid question?'

Go on, I said.
'What is a podcast?'

We both had a good laugh once I heard the question. Not because it was a bad question. But because we both had two different lenses that we were operating with.

I explained what a podcast was. Once she realized it was pretty much a personal radio show, that's when she got really hyped!

So, what was the lesson?

The lesson was, **sometimes, you have to over communicate.**

In my world, a 'podcast' is a regular terminology. But in her world, 'radio' is a regular terminology.

Therefore, it was not right of me to assume she knew what it was.

The tricky thing about over communicating is knowing WHEN to do it. There's a fine line.

Over communicating every little sentence will put people to sleep and will cause rambling.

'So how do I know WHEN to over communicate?'
By analyzing body language.

There are tons of individuals in the social world who do not want to directly say something because they fear they will come off as rude, or their question is stupid.

Therefore, the ball is in the court of the communicator to look out for sudden shifts in the body which seem out of the ordinary.

In my situation, my client kept looking to the side, touching her neck & seemed like she wanted to ask me a question. That told me that something was up.

Our body has a special kind of intelligence built in it. A lot of times, our body will alert us when the vibe is not congruent.

Let me give you a dummies' version of what I'm talking about. Check this out:

When you see out of character body movements, start asking questions & over communicating.

Let's say you are the person in a conversation who doesn't understand a certain concept, then what?

'I feel like the answer is very simple.'
It is.

Stop the other person and ask them to explain.
Don't assume they can tell something is wrong.

Most people don't know how to read bodies.
Only a few people do.

If they are a stand-up person, then they will clarify without hesitation. If they make a fuss out of an innocent question, then that's a character flaw. You should think twice before working with someone like that.

The body gives clues that words bury.

That's because the internal world is solidified in the body language.
'Can I unlock a 6th sense?'
Sure. By becoming fluent in body language.

Ðealing with Bad Ðays

Bad days...
Good days...
Common among everyone under the sun.

A couple years back, I had a job interview coming up. Up until this point, I had gotten rejected from multiple internship opportunities.

Do you have any engineering experience?' they would ask.

I'd wonder, how the hell am I supposed to have experience if this was going to be my first ever engineering job??

After a series of failures, I finally got a call back from this medical equipment company. They were hiring engineers. And they needed engineers ASAP.

They asked if I could be ready for an interview the next day. This was very low preparation time, but I didn't have any other choice.

So, I said yes.

I studied up on the company & wished for the best.

The next day arrived.

My appointment was scheduled at 6pm. But something strange started happening around 3pm.
'What?'
I started getting very sleepy.

I wasn't a big coffee guy around that time, so decided to take a power nap for 20 minutes. I'm sure you are picking up what happened next.

'Uh, overslept?'

Yep.

My brother wakes me up at 5pm to see if I still had the interview. I woke up shocked to see that I had overslept so long!!

The alarm had been set for 3:20 am rather than 3:20 pm.

I put on a wrinkly ass dress shirt & pants, then ran to the bus station.

As I'm waiting for the bus, I notice a car driving along the road right by me. On top of this car's roof, I see a big jug of water. Clearly, the car owner forgot to take his jug of water off the roof.

 As the car's speed picked up, the jug went flying aimed at my direction.

There was no time to adjust.

The jug slammed onto the ground and soaked me from waist down. To make matters worse... **It wasn't water.**

This driver was probably headed to the gym and probably put some protein in the water or something. I don't know. But only thing I did know was that I was STICKY.

Nasty as hell.

By the time I got to the interview, I was still sleepy, had

wrinkly clothes on & was sticky from some random liquid. To make it worse, I was livid.

Although my words may have been 'right' during the interview, my attitude was sour. I let my vibe get ruined. The elder gentlemen in his 50s, could sense my attitude.

'How do you know he could tell?'
I'm not sure. But I think it was just something about his body language which showed that he noticed.

He gave me the impression of: *'not sure if I want this kid working for me. He has bad vibes.'*

I didn't end up getting the job but I learned a few lessons that day.

The lessons were:

o   Anything random can happen.
o   People who seem agitated may have encountered dark events leading up to your encounter. So don't personalize it.
o   Iron your clothes beforehand.
o   Learn to control your attitude.

The last lesson was probably the most significant.

And that's what made an engineer of 5+ years curious about the world of emotional intelligence.

I wanted to learn if I could control my emotions.

I spent so many years as an electrical engineer playing with electricity. But came to notice that emotions are remarkably similar to electricity. Humans are very intricate machines.

The main takeaway is that emotional intelligence is exercise during dark times.

At this day in age, we can do it during dark AND light times.

Many of us don't know how to take a win.
'You mean how to take a loss?'
No, a win.

Once we win, we automatically undermine it, never acknowledge it or just go chasing for another win.

Leveling up is great. However, learning to be grateful is how we ensure more wins. Bad days allow you to exercise your internal world.

Just imagine, what an intense internal workout it would have been to be enthusiastic DESPITE feeling sleepy, wearing wrinkly clothes & being soaked from some random substance.

Practicing emotional intelligence is how Ls are turned into Ws.

When the internal world is strengthened to overpower the external world, others can feel your presence.

This isn't the fake persona you put on to be some tough guy. Instead, it stems from a deeper power that doesn't exist in the material world.

What separates cocky and confidence?

Cocky people try to earn praise.

Confident people don't give a fuck.

Is Positive Thinking Bad?

Positive thinking is not necessarily bad. It's a good steppingstone to loosen the grip of negative thinking.

But what's more powerful than positive thinking is acceptance as a whole.
This is what gives a strong attitude.

Learning meditation in college was confusing.
I accidentally stumbled into it one day. The story is long. So don't want to get into that.

As a novice meditator, I thought the goal was to shut off the mind. Thought the goal was to be empty. Tried that a few times. But it didn't work for me.

During my time trying to shut off thoughts, I noticed something.
'What?'
A lot of thoughts are nonsense.

Meaning, that they are completely random. Some serve utility. But a lot of thoughts are just random.

As I got older, I realized meditation is best when you do not try to eliminate thoughts.
Rather, you learn to co-exist with your thoughts.

Positive & negative thoughts are welcomed.
In either case, acceptance is met.

This sounds all cool & loving, but what practical use can I get from this in terms of my communication?

Plenty.

You'll notice right before you get called on stage to give a speech, that is when you may have your most negative thoughts. When you are a newbie speaker.

Be the speaker that just accepts whatever. The good, the bad, does not matter.

Hoping only for positive thoughts will make you nervous. Because at times, you may not have full control.

What's funny is that a big part of mind
management is learning to make a joke out of the mind.

Let's say you have a mean boss who yells a lot.
At first, when he yells, you are very scared.
Even sad.

But as time passes by, you see that this boss yells at times.
Is happy at times.
Is confused at times.
Is lazy at times.
You start to understand this boss on a deeper level.

As time passes by, you start to build a bond with this boss.
You've seen the good & the bad of his personality.

So, the next time they yell, the new co-worker may be scared.
But you will be like, 'that's just Bill being Bill haha.'

That's how it works with the mind.
We take it less seriously to gain more power over it.

When you just want positive thoughts, you lowkey condition yourself as a victim.
Why?
Because it's the nature of the mind to give positive, negative & random thoughts.

The goal of leveling up is to be more powerful than the thoughts.

The more power you gain over it through acceptance, the more your thoughts can serve practical purpose.

Same with a lot of us who have smartphones. Often, we can spot garbage from a mile away.
If you have a semblance of media literacy, you can spot propaganda with ease.

So, we spot the negative content and accept that it exists behind the screen. While us, the human, remains unaffected. Allowing us to move on.

But if you say something silly like:
'Oh no, I see a propaganda piece on my phone. The propaganda piece is negative. And since it is on my phone, then I must be negative too!'
Then you will be living a very turbulent life.

Remember this...
If the good opinions get to your head.
Then the mean opinions get to your heart.

Remain unaffected.

Take away power from your mind to gain mastery over your mind.

Was positive thinking bad?

Not quite.

But the coin has 2 sides.

-Rather than seeing heads or tails, see the coin.

-Rather than seeing the waves, see the ocean.

-Rather than seeing diversity, see the unity that rests behind all that.

The Storytelling Ego

Imagine that you just got out of work & are driving home. You had a long day, so you are just chilling & driving.

As you are in the zone, out of nowhere, you see there is a car tailgating you. It's one of those aggressive tailgaters.

The driver gets as close as they can without hitting you.

You look around the other lanes & see that it's empty. So you have no clue why this person doesn't just go around you.

You're just chilling. No way in hell are you going be the one moving out of the tailgaters way.

The tailgater gets even closer.

Eventually, he gets fed up & goes to the other lane to overtake you.

But he doesn't overtake you in a gentle way. Instead, he cuts you off so close that he almost hits the front of your car!

Now you are pissed.

Here you were 3 minutes ago relaxing & not bothering anyone. Now out of nowhere, this clown came & is actively ruining your day.

The untamed ego is deciding whether it should come out to play.

At this point, you have 2 choices.

1. Tailgate this person & give him a taste of his own medicine.
Or
2. Ignore.

'Ignore Armani??? Get the fuck out of here! He just ruined my day. He isn't getting off so easy!'

What if I told you that you have something to gain by letting him off the hook?

'I'd call you a liar!'
Well, there *is* something that you will gain.
'What is it?'
The ability to tell a story.

'Huh?'
To understand what I mean by this, you need to know what the ego is.

The ego is a dualistic force.
It sees right or wrong.
Neutral is not in its vocabulary.

The ego creates your sense of identity. It shapes a lot of your reality, whether you are aware or not. People with an untamed ego typically lack awareness.

'So how does all this help me become a better storyteller?'
Well, in the example of the tailgater, guess what your ego is doing?
'What?'
It is creating a narrative.

The villain: tailgater.

Conflict: being tailgated.
Resolution: ??

This narrative has a character, conflict & a potential resolution. What does that sound like?
'Holy shit, a story!'

Your ego is presenting stories to you all day. That's why I believe storytelling is primal. It's a part of our nature.

The question is, are the stories being used destructively or constructively?

Destructively is when you tailgate the other person back and give the ego what it wants. After, you feel drained.

You have this bitter attitude & snap at anyone that talks to you. The ego now has a stronger grip over you.

-Short term pleasure for long term pain.

Constructively is when you write the story on a journal or blog. You **externalize** it. Take the material from the internal to the external. This makes it real.

When you do this, you have loosened the grip of the ego over your reality. Now you are not in the mercy of outside circumstances.

Sure, you had to let the tailgater slide. But now you feel more whole.

-Short term pain for long term pleasure.

The ego is a vehicle for infinite content for a personal brand, YouTube channel, podcast, book and much more. However, if you choose to just react to it, your mind will always be running amuck.

Emotions come and go but the consequences can come and stay.

The storytelling ego is a weapon in my eyes.

Fearlessness

I had this little cousin who used to be terrified of ghosts. When I mean terrified... I mean he was scared shitless. *His name was Raehan.*

My brother and I noticed that he would normally get scared at the nighttime. But in the daytime? It was harder to scare him.

One day, Raehan came to our house in the daytime... And my brother and I set a bet on who could scare him first.

We were little kids. My brother was 13 & I was 11. Raehan was 7.

I was first up.

I told him a story about how there is a ghost that lives right outside our house and that he should be scared.

Tried to milk the story for a while but Raehan wasn't budging. Kid really felt bold in the daytime, I see. The story definitely would have worked at night!

My brother was next up.
He piggybacked off my story but made it more believable.

15 minutes passed on by and I could hear Raehan crying!

Damn...
So, I lost the bet.

I wondered why this happened? Was it because the story was more believable or because Raehan was a chicken?

As I get older, I know Raehan wouldn't be scared of ghost stories anymore. The kid is 24 years old now. That would be pathetic.

What changed?
'His age bro.'
Nope. His perception.

There is a big mistake we make where we say the older someone is, the more mature they are.
That's not always the case.

Sometimes you'll see an older person making an ass out of themselves, while someone a whole decade younger is more composed.

Maturity is a game of perception.

Same with fear.
It's a game of warping the perception over time. Age and years have little to do with it.

This is a significant point to understand. Very significant.
'Why?'
Because confusing the 2 will have you wasting time.

I used to be scared of speaking up. Was shy for many years of my life.

I had the illusion that the fear would go away with time.

Thought shyness would melt away on its own.

As years started to pass on by, I realized that was not the case. I just got older but was not fearless.

The day I decided to take my butt to Toastmasters was the day I realized that shyness needed to be CONSCIOUSLY worked on. And that, it was.

Why do we do self-improvement in the first place?
'Uh....'

Gravity does not only exist for the body.
Gravity also exists for the mind.

Just like the gravitational pull, PULLS our bodies down. It aims to pull our mind down as well.

Which is why unless you take care of the mind and constantly learn to sharpen it, it starts to become dull.

Meaning that self-improvement is FIGHTING against gravity.
Don't you wonder why you are doing it?

'Why am I doing it bro?'
You are doing it to become fearless.

'That seems like a bold goal!'
It is.

However, that bold goal is what turns potential energy into kinetic energy and you begin starting your journey rather than saying 'I'll do it tomorrow.'

The bold goal also HELPS fight the gravitational pull. You break through different stratospheres.

I love the universe picture. I have a poster of it in my living room, it's my phone background, and if you check out my YouTube, it's in the studio setup.

The universe allows the mind to be OPEN.
It allows the mind to feel limitless.

Limitless and fearlessness are one in the same.

It's a bold goal but this bold goal allows one to MOVE.

Discipline is boring if you are just doing a bunch of random acts. However, if you have a narrative behind those acts, then it becomes a game.

All self-improvement comes down to is becoming better than you were yesterday.
You feel bold because you put in the work.

People enter self-improvement via different vehicles.
-Some do it via eCommerce.
-Others do it via pick up artistry.
-There are people who do it via fitness.
-My brand does it via communication skills.

The target is the same.
The target is to become fearless.

Addictions

How do we control addictions?
Do we stop cold turkey, or to we ease ourselves out of it?

I had a friend from college who became an alcoholic when he graduated from undergrad. The guy had a lot of pressure dealing with law school & being in his profession.

One time, he invited me into his law school where he had to do a mock trial.

For law school, there is a class where you prepare the entire semester to be part of a trial.
You are presented with a case. Given a judge. Witnesses and all that.

This was dope. I was invited to be a part of the audience and watch.

As I was watching my friend in action, talking about why his 'client' was innocent...I noticed something.
'What?'
He seemed a little loud.

Maybe he was getting in the lawyer zone.
But maybe it was something else.

I've seen him in our undergrad parties before.
Can tell when he has had a little too much to drink. He gets loud.

The tone he had in the mock trial sounded strangely similar to our undergrad moments.

Others thought he was in the zone. I thought I'd give him the benefit of the doubt.

Once the trial was over, a few of us went to the back to meet up with the mock trial participants. As soon as I greeted this friend...
I got a strong whiff of Jack Daniels.

Yea.
He had been doing this case tipsy or drunk.

That was one of the memories I had of him before he went to seek help. Before he admitted to himself that he was an alcoholic.

I feel for him.

When I was young, I wondered why people didn't just stop. Could it be that hard?

But that's when he was saying he feels STRONG sensations in his body when he just tries stopping. He starts shaking & goes through insomnia.

You learn something new every day. Seeing this friend go through alcoholism showed me to be more understanding when someone is battling addiction.

It seems easy from the outside. Difficult when you're actually going through it.

One thing I recall him doing was easing himself out of alcohol.
Where he would not quit cold turkey but gradually do less & less.

To take it a level further, he had an accountability buddy, support system & app that measured how many days he went without alcohol once he was in his groove.

When he saw the days piling up, everything felt more REAL. Overcoming this addiction was doing wonders for his confidence.

This story isn't about telling you to quit alcohol.
Instead, it's to showcase insights regarding addiction.

There are different forms of addictions that different people face. The mind has the tendency to make us overdo something at certain times. Whether it's an addiction with porn, alcohol, social media, sweets etc.

It's good to remain aware of how others are going through addictions. Doing some research to keep your mind aware of this niche of information.

There are frameworks that have been designed so you can move with more clarity if you ever stumble upon it at a certain moment.

Never say 'that could never happen to me.'
Life has a way of proving us wrong.

Practice

No matter which skillset it is, practice will be the barrier of entry.

If practice is so important, then there should be a clear definition for it. What's your definition?
'To repetitively do something.'

You gave me 4 words.
'What do you think?'
It's okay, but not great.

'So what's your definition smart guy?'
Rewire the nervous system.
I believe these 4 words gives a more concrete understanding.

Practice turns a trained act into an instinct.
And to do that:
A task needs to be done mindfully before it can be done mindlessly.
Key word is: "before."

Doing the task mindlessly from the get-go sets up the practice session to be a failure.

Simply valuing repetition undermines the role of the mind.

'What does that mean?'
That means you are physically in the practice session, but the mind is in Disneyland.

Mechanical moves without presence leads to the session becoming much **less effective.**

By including "nervous system" in the definition of practice, things change. I don't know about you, but the phrase 'nervous system' seems like an important phrase to me.

The nervous system consists of:
Central: brain & spine.
Peripheral: nerves (sensory & motor).

We are information beings.
Constantly passing information from one end to the next.

'Do I need to learn anything in particular to rewire the nervous system?'
How about you take a walk down memory lane?

There have been plenty of times in our lives when we rewired ourselves internally.
When we learned to brush our teeth.
Type.
Drive.
And learn anything.

Anytime something is learned with the mind being present, new connections are fired in the brain. The study of neuroplasticity has shown that the brain is not fixed for life. It is capable of being molded like Play Doh.

With the 'rewiring our nervous system' definition for practice, repetition becomes a byproduct. But this time, these are not mindless repetitions.

It's the mindful repetitions.

Another variable that plays a role in the practice session are the stakes. High stakes or low stakes?

Example:
Brushing our teeth = Low Stake
Therefore, the mind is given more freedom to be mindless.
Learning to drive = High Stake
Therefore, the mind is given less freedom to be mindless.

How can someone increase the level of presence for tasks which seem low stake? Like writing.

It's easy to become mindless because you technically will not die if you allow yourself to be mindless.

In cases like this, the timer is the best friend.

Something about a timer counting down the time simulates the effects of a HIGH-STAKE situation out of a low-stake one.

With this renewed narrative, it is much easier to place yourself in a state of a mindful attitude.
And then repetitively rewire the nervous system.

The whole purpose of practice is to turn a trained act to an instinct. No matter if it's with a speech, listening, or writing skills.

Behavior sharpens when a clarified definition is introduced. 4 words:
Rewire the nervous system.

Grant Cardone Vs. Jordan Belfort

There is this podcast with Grant Cardone & Jordan Belfort that is available on YouTube. 2 legends in the sales game.

This collaboration should be a peaceful discussion with tons of takeaways, right?
Wrong.

This interaction turned into a heated debate.
Two titans locking horns.

Grant Cardone has built his career being the King of Sales. But on this podcast? Something strange had happened.

He was talking in circles.

Jordan (who you know as the character from Wolf on Wall Street) would ask him plenty of straightforward questions, but Grant would start dancing around the answer.

It was stunning to watch.

This was an awful look for Grant considering that he had insulted Jordan in the past by calling him a rip-off.

In this episode, it seemed as like Jordan was clearly more skilled in sales, not even close.

Is he though?
That's up for debate.

But if you read the comment section of the interview, the perception is a LANDSLIDE win in favor of Jordan.

So what happened to Uncle G?

Grant made a TON of communication errors in this podcast. I've watched him for many years & have never seen his game off by that big of a margin. Let's go through a few social errors.

1. He wouldn't shut the fuck up

One of the most annoying habits of Grant Cardone & Gary Vee is that they interrupt a lot.

It's like they are allergic to letting the other person finish a point before interjecting. Grant did this MULTIPLE times.

I think I counted Jordan finishing less than 10 thoughts in the entire interview.

This made Grant come off as very rude.

On the other hand, Jordan was more tamed & let Grant talk.

2. A lot of insults flying

Grant has this cunning way of insulting someone with a smile on his face. So, he comes off as friendly while dissing his target.

He said Jordan's friends were druggies, implied he was a bad interviewer, and said Jordan was too focused on 'tricks.'

Anytime Grant was asked a reasonable question, he got

defensive.

His body language showed how uncomfortable he was.

He was trying to bully Jordan, but it was not remotely working.

Jordan maintained composure & would laugh off the attacks without taking the bait. That gave him more social points.

3. Not being clear

Grant was saying a lot of sentences that didn't make any sense in the interview.

Anytime Jordan would ask him for practical strategies, he would give some cryptic responses.

One weird line was: *'when someone is not interested, it means they are interested.'*

I guess it makes sense if you watch Grant's content. But this was Jordan's podcast. Therefore, it's important to communicate in a way where the new audience is able to keep up.

The lack of direct responses made him look like a typical 'internet guru' who lacks depth. But that's sad because Grant isn't like that.

Grant made a follow up video after the interview saying that he wasn't detailed about the sales questions because his philosophy had changed.

He now believes you should focus more on marketing and building your brand which allows the sales process to be smoother.

Great viewpoint. But you need to be clear fam!!

4. Very egotistical.

Grant is a 10x thinker. So, he doesn't think like most people out there. I get it.

But he was coming off as very egotistical.

He kept bringing up his successes as a reason to not explain himself.

Imagine if you wanted some practical tips from me in terms of communication skills & I kept saying, 'I'm a Toastmaster champ.'

You'll think, 'cool, now can you answer my question?'

That's how it felt watching this interview.

Overall, this was a poor look for Uncle G. But this just goes to show, *even the best of us have bad days.*

This is by no means an attack on Grant Cardone's character. He is a stellar guy & his work has tremendously benefited my life.

This breakdown is simply an objective evaluation of what I saw.

Hopefully, you can watch the interview & read this breakdown to understand how NOT to carry yourself in a social interaction.

By knowing what not to do, it's easier to find out what to do.

Where Elvis Presley Went Wrong

I once heard 2 people arguing about who was bigger in their time:

Elvis Presley or Michael Jackson.

The debate was getting huge with each side putting up their own points.

Soon enough, a 3rd person came & said they were arguing about 2 different things.

Elvis was the King of Rock.
Michael was the King of Pop.

No need to compare. The debate fizzled out after that.

I'll be honest...I don't know much about Elvis. I know a lot about Michael Jackson considering I've listened to a lot of his songs.

But with Elvis? Only heard about him from Uncle Jesse in Full house.

So, I watched a documentary on him recently and was left feeling inspired.

He had a unique style which allowed him to have a quick meteoric rise.

Until he fell off from grace due to outdated song styles.

But luckily, he was one of the *few* artists who was able to launch a comeback & finish off with a bang.

Unfortunately, he didn't **fully** end his career in a bang. He became fat, began doing drugs & hated performing nonstop in Vegas.

As I looked closer, I saw why that was.

Elvis had a manager who used him to profit off him.

Did the manager open a lot of doors for Elvis?
Of course.

But did he also take advantage of Elvis?
Unfortunately, yes.

His manager prevented him from launching a lot of creative songs because it broke the mold of what the record labels wanted.

For a big part of his life, Elvis was stifled due to this manager. That's unfortunately the pain Elvis dealt with.
A creative genius who was stifled by authority.

I'm a firm believer of cutting out complexity with creative content. Which is why I salute independent artists who make a living. They do not need a record label watering their stuff down.

As my brand grows, I will outsource a lot of tasks. But one thing I will never outsource is the content.

That's a communication sin in my eyes.

Do you possess a creative talent?
Whether it's comedy, cooking, singing, storytelling, public speaking, etc.

If so, I recommend you double down on it & keep away from the profit vultures.

With the rise of social media, our generation has what Elvis did not have.
'What is that?'
The power over our own narrative.

We don't need some corporation telling us what to do. We can keep our businesses lean & follow our intuition.

How have you been leveraging your creative talents?

If you have been thinking about sharing your talents, but have been overthinking...

Then stop thinking so much & just do.

Simply view the creative act as a hobby rather than a channel to build followers. That's how you maintain your authenticity.

We are living in the golden era of creativity.
Now, there is **power** to build a global brand with consistency & a little bit of strategy.

Intuition

You ever noticed there are a few things we all do?
'Can you give me an example?'
Yes. Flinching.

You ever had that moment when your friend was pretending
like they were going to hit you & you flinched?

Or what about when your body flinched mid nap because you
thought you were about to fall off a cliff?

I never really knew what intuition was. Your boy was a
logical fellow growing up. I needed rational, logic & facts for
me to make up my mind. Everything else was biased or not
worth my time.

Nowadays, things have changed.
Nowadays, I am more intuitive.

'What changed?'
Experience.

When learning something, logic is needed. Logic is what
helps grasp the fundamentals.

When learning the fundamentals, being robotic is fine.

Once the fundamentals have been grasped, now it's time to
create our own rules.
Example: Driving.

We all learned driving in a similar way.

Quite sure it was in a quiet location or park, where we got acclimated with the steering wheel, accelerator, brakes, and all that. *The fundamentals.*

But nowadays, we all have our own unique brand of driving. Some are fast drivers, some slow, some follow the speed limit to the tee & some get road rage like they are paid for it.

Ultimately, you learn the rules & then you bend them. That's a logical to creative transformation.

Like an artist who learns how to mix colors and how to sketch before they begin creating anything that comes to their mind.

Only 1 MAJOR creative transformation can completely shift the paradigm.

That's when you begin viewing life differently.

Nowadays, we dissect first and skip the beauty. Always looking for flaws, what ifs & loopholes. But that's the wrong mindset for intuition.

See the beauty first and then dissect when needed.

At the end of the day, logic to intuition is a spectrum. It's not one or the other.

You should not JUST be logical or JUST be intuitive. Instead, it is more of a balancing act.

Life Irony:
It takes intuition to know when you need to listen to your intuition.

Gut instinct is primal for the body.
Curiosity is primal for the mind.

I often feel as though we were born with the answers within
and it just takes the right questions to connect the dots.

I have no proof of this. But then again....
That may be my intuition talking.

The Butterfly Effect

When I was working in IT, my team was managing a system for USCIS. It was a very complex system with TONS of moving parts. Difficult to manage.

One day, we had a small bug in the system. It was **very** small. So small to a point where we thought it was no biggie. Decided to ignore it.

4 Months Later...

I'm sleeping on a Saturday morning, until I get a call at 6:40 am. It's my manager.

He says 'Armani, we need you at work ASAP. We have a p1!'

A p1 is when our system is in a **critical state.** On the verge of failure. This causes our company to miss deadlines & clients to get pissed. This was bad.

We ended up working a fuck ton the next week. 12 hours a day with the business analysts, systems engineers, infrastructure engineers etc. to find the root cause.

After a few weeks, we found out what happened.

'What happened bro?'
You remember that *little* bug that I decided to ignore a few months back?
'Yea.'
Well, that bug had compounded over time & turned into a freaking monster. That was the reason our system almost

collapsed.

The butterfly effect is the concept that a flap of a butterfly's wings can add up, compound exponentially & lead to a tornado on the other side of the world.

This is nonlinear thinking.

Little things are often ignored. But it is the little things that lead to the big things. Remember the butterfly effect when you sleep on little things.

Machines & people have certain similarities.

It's like if we can learn how a machine functions or destructs, we can about ourselves in the process.

That day of covering up the small bug led to a p1. That's when the concept of the butterfly effect became crystallized.

Has a small thing ever led to a big thing in YOUR life? Answer the question.

You'll be surprised by the responses.

Why Some People Just Don't Get it

Have you ever tried explaining something to someone who was doubtful?
It's a pain in the ass.

It seems like you are saying all the right things.
But the person just doesn't get it.

This is because of a concept known as "cognitive complexity."

Cognitive complexity is used differently in fields.
'What is it?'
Cognitive complexity is a person's ability to process information.

Some people can process information at very high rates. They are what we call nuanced thinkers. Some people process information at terribly slow or medium rates.

If you consider yourself a cognitive complex thinker and you know you are talking to someone who may be a bit slow to process information, then:

-You should NOT try to show off your cognitive complexity.
-Instead, you should redirect the conversation, ignore the conversation, or simplify your complexity.

We are all cognitive complex in certain fields and simple in others.

If someone talks to me about Hollywood gossip, I will have no clue what they are saying. But if they talk to me about Hollywood movies, I will have a clue.

It's a matter of shifting focus.

Great communicators reduce their tendency to judge.

It's easy to be like, *'look how much smarter I am than this poor fellow.'*
This is a poor habit.

The more you do this, the more you condition a sense of separateness from the world. This behavior will amplify anxiety & lead to an aggressive communication style.

Humans are brands. Each brand represents a different order of values.

When you go in with the understanding that you can learn from ANYONE, that's when your cognitive complexity is seen as a gift, not a curse.

You don't want to be one of those smart people with poor social skills.

If you consider yourself intelligent, you may often feel like others should catch up to your level but that's the ego talking.

It takes a HIGH level of intelligence to have clarity in your message.
So much clarity that nonnative speakers can even follow your words with ease.

People carry a whole bunch of beliefs, attitudes, and values
with them.
- o   So, you are rarely ONLY communicating with
      someone's present self.
- o   You are communicating with their past view of
      themselves, present & future ambitions.

When you realize humans are processing information from
ALL aspects of their life, that's when it's easier to understand
why some people just don't get it.

All good.

Everyone doesn't need to get it. If everyone gets your
message, then you are probably just spitting platitudes. No
matter how simple you speak, some will get it, but not agree.

All good.

Realize that everyone's cognitive complexity is different, and
their ambitions are different as well.

And when miscommunication does happen, you finetune
what is in your control & ignore the rest.

If you read the line above, that's also a recipe for thick skin.

Spotting the Silver Lining

The year was 2014. I just graduated from college. It was my time to go out into the real world.

'Did you have any certain plans?'
Yes. I was offered a job in Virginia.

The job was as a process engineer for Capital One. My team would deal with creating global investment tools for the firm.

The pay that they were offering seemed surreal to me. Very high. Everything seemed to be lining up.

But deep inside, something felt off.

Is this really happening?

Am I really going to move out of Florida for this job? Leave my family? Abandon all my friends? Start over in a new state?

The whole decision process was nerve-wracking.
A part of me did not want to enter this new territory of life.

But the other part of me knew that I needed to move in order to grow. I had spent my entire life in Florida. I needed a change of scenery.

Decisions, decisions.

Final Answer

I decided to accept the role. Informed all my friends & family.

'Were they upset?'
Yes. But they knew that it was necessary.

All my loved ones ended up throwing me a surprise going away party the night before my flight. It was such a kind act by them.

I was sad knowing that I could not see these people at whim any longer. But I could not mope around. This was an excellent opportunity and I needed to be happy for myself.

Flight Time

The party was excellent. I was reminiscing about all the fun moments of the night the next morning when I was about to enter my flight.
My parents & my brother accompanied me to the airport.

Before I was about to enter the flight, both my parents wanted to give me a final few words.

My dad was first up.

'Son, listen. You are about to start a brand-new journey for your life. You are going to be completely responsible for your actions. Remember, you come from a generation of respectable people. Never forget your roots. Maintain your honor at all times. Even when no one is watching.'

Yes dad.

Next up was my mom.

'Listen, son. I want you to know one thing. You may be moving away. But you will always be my baby boy. I love you so much. My heart is broken knowing that you will not be in the same state as me. But I know you will make me proud.'

She broke down in tears.

My brother was pretty quiet. He did not say much.

'Tampa to Dulles Airport. Please begin boarding.'

Well, it was time. I hugged my loved ones. Said goodbye. And went off to begin my new journey.

6 months later

It started off as a bumpy ride but Virginia was not bad at all.

I was able to get accustomed to life very quickly due to having some fraternity brothers living in the state.

We explored the city, did road trips, met some cuties, all the fun stuff. Life here was not too bad.

'What about your job? How was that?'
Good question.

I learned a lot from that job. The role taught me how to design data structures and increase process efficiency for global trading tools.

My team got me caught up & had me feeling like I was at home. The company culture was great.

But...
'But, what?'

The Grinch

My boss was tough. Not some 'tough but fair' stuff. This man was a bitter fuck who hated his role.

This man would bring his personal problems into the work environment. He was getting a divorce & you could tell it was taking a toll on his emotions & logic.

He made it a habit of yelling at his team and throwing hissy fits when things didn't go his way. No clue how that clown was made a manager in the first place.

Oh well, nothing that I can't deal with. Well, at least that's what I thought.

However, one day I reached a breaking point.

The day of the snow

It was snowing very badly one morning. At one moment, I was amazed.

Your boy was from Florida. This was my first-time seeing

snow.
You know damn well I had to Snapchat this moment.

'Did you run outside and make a snow angel too??'
Hell no. Let's not go too far.

But I was a little confused. The snow was slowing down.

Do I go to work? I'm from the sunshine city.
I do not know how all this stuff works in a snowy city. This is
the perfect situation for me to work from home, right?

Wrong.

I called my boss to see if it was okay to work from home.

Nope.

My boss wanted me to go to the office. He was not a fan of
the whole 'work from home' thing unless it was an
emergency.

I was very shocked by his lack of consideration. It did not
seem remotely safe to drive in that snow.

Oh well.

So, I got ready & began to set out for mission impossible.

Emptier than a party that ran out of booze

The roads were completely empty. NO ONE was driving.

Why am I driving?

I was taking it very slowly, but something did not feel right. Maybe I am just being paranoid.

Decided I might as well listen to some music rather than mope around.

Still, something was feeling very strange.

Car steering wheel was shaking a lot. My engine seemed louder than normal. The tread in my tires seemed like it had weakened.

No Armani, stop. You are just being paranoid.

Then... BOOOM!!

My car starts losing control.

Oh no. I hit black ice.

(Black ice is the ice that blends in with the road and is not easy to spot. Very deadly. It can make your vehicle lose full control.)

My car started swerving. I was doing my best to control the steering wheel to get back on the path. But no luck. No luck at all.

My car was spinning out of control.
Screeching noise.
Tire smoke.

Loose steering wheel.

The car was now spinning in circles. Oh no.. I'm about to hit the side of the bridge. The bridge was right above a body of water.

Get control dammit.
Get control!

You are in trouble if you do not make something happen.

Come on, come on, come on Armani...

CONCENTRATE.

Make something happen.
Please...

The moment my life flashed

Not sure what happened.

I was able to gain back control of my car to brake in the very last second.

I kid you not. The car hit the railing of the bridge. The railing alone is what saved me from having my car fly into the ocean.

This was a MIRACLE. And trust me, I do not use that word casually.

My taillight was busted. But everything was okay.

But was it really okay?

What if there were other cars on the road?
What if I wasn't able to brake the car?
What if I had gotten in a fatal car accident?

The questions began running through my mind. I was pissed
that I was supposed to be going into the office.

My manager's face popped up in my mind and I boiled with
anger.

Stop.
I survived.
This is a great opportunity to be grateful.
I will drive extra slow to the office.

Guys..?

I finally got to the office and guess what? It was
COMPLETELY empty.

Not even my fatass manager was there. Only me.

Okay no more being grateful. Back to being mad.

Not a single person? I almost died.

And everyone is working from the comfort of their own
homes, drinking coffee & chilling. While I was here worrying
about my long drive back home.

This is bullshit.

The birth of an epiphany

At that moment, I knew that something was not right. Something needed to change. I needed more control.

You know what? I know I am an engineer. But whatever. I will one day figure out the business world. I will combine my engineering talent with business. I did not want some fat fuck with 0 empathy telling me what to do anymore.

The love for engineering was still there. But why not enhance my engineering and learn business on the side?

Who knows, there is a small chance that I could combine the two?

'Technology meets business.' Doesn't sound bad at all.

A few years later

Since that near-death experience, I have been involved in many spaces of online business.

I have done Amazon white label, virtual real estate, owned an Instagram sports entertainment site, did global popup & banner marketing etc.
I have lost money, gained money, learned lessons and I am still not done. I am a work in progress in the business world.

It will all be figured out.

So what?

That near death car accident was awful at first, yes. I was
terrified, angry, upset all at the same damn time.

My perception only focused on the negatives during that
moment.

However, after looking back in hindsight, that moment alone
guided me in my journey. The moment sparked my interest
in entrepreneurship.

That moment alone led me onto my path
in entrepreneurship for the last several years.

If that near-death car accident never happened, guess what?
'What?'
I would have probably been only focused on engineering &
have had 0 side projects.

By no means am I where I want to be in my engineering and
business career.
There is a lot of work to be done. But need to start off
somewhere, right?

Spotting the the silver lining

The point is that some of the darkest moments in your life
have a silver lining buried within it.

It is your goal to discover that silver lining.

My near-death experience in that car ride was not simply

a reason to be upset with my boss.

It was the first experience that sparked my
interest in entrepreneurship. It sparked an
internal curiosity for the mysterious world of business.

Those were my personal takeaways from that experience.

Nowadays, I look back at that moment and laugh at how
funny life is. So can you.

My challenge to you

Anytime you are pissed, go on and let yourself feel heated.
You are human.

No need to hide it.
But when you have cooled off, ask yourself:
'What is the silver lining?'

- o *Is there a lesson that I can learn from this
  experience?*
- o *Is this experience guiding me to a new perspective?*

Be more curious about your experiences. Do not just get
pissed and throw a hissy fit.

Your experiences alone are worth more than any words
another man or woman will tell you.
'Why?'
Because you have actually lived it.

It really is never that bad

Despite the darkest clouds in life, know one thing. With time, the pain will melt.

I was able to make this realization with many of the trauma's I faced in life.

No matter how hard, keep looking to find the good in the bad. This will be VERY tough at first.

But no one said spotting the silver lining was going to be easy. That is why most people do not bother to do it. Each time you spot the silver lining, each time you rewire your subconscious minds to see the positive.

A positive mind will lead to positive thinking.

Positive thinking will lead to positive actions.

Positive actions will lead to a positive feeling.

That's will spotting the silver lining will be a habit rather than something that requires conscious effort.

Leverage

I was at work. Bored out of my mind.

To make matters worse, I was stuck with busy work. I had to copy and paste a bunch of numbers from one document into a system.

My manager asked me & my coworker Dennis to have it done before the day. There were 1000 numbers. When split, I had to do 500 & Dennis had to do 500.

As we began, I highlighted the numbers, clicked Control C (copy) + Control V (paste).

Dennis manually highlighted the numbers, hit right click on his mouse, clicked copy, and then clicked paste.

I was in my early 20s at the time and Dennis was in his early 50s.

Clearly from our methods, you could see the difference in our approach.

My task was done in 35 minutes. Dennis took 2 hours.

It was a very small change in methods. But the results were staggering.

When Dennis asked me how I got done so fast, I showed him the keyboard shortcuts.

He looked at it like I was speaking some foreign language. Even though my method had LESS physical steps, Dennis blurts out:

'I can't do that. I'm just going to go with my method.'

Dennis was one of my favorite coworkers. He showed me the ropes when I just got hired. However, seeing him stuck in his old ways made me sad.

The digital divide is the divide between those who have access to computers/internet and those who do not.

To extend on the definition, I'd also add, those who have FLUENCY in computers/internet and those who do not.

Dennis grew up in a different era than I did. A world where anything digital was seen as a fad. Nowadays, digital is taking a tighter grip over our lives.

Leverage in its most fundamental definition is **to use something to its maximum advantage.**

Fluency in technology is just one form of leverage.

A simple change in keystrokes can save *tons* of time. All time that can be reinvested into doing something else.

'What's another form of leverage bro?'
Another form of leverage is experience.

If you're someone who plays pickup basketball, you may have seen that one old timer schooling a bunch of the young bucks.

Why? The young bucks are full of energy and athleticism.

Yes, but the old timer has played several of pickup games in his life. He has minimal wasted movements. When he does make a move, it's well thought out. Consciously or subconsciously.

In this case, experience is leverage.

'Gotcha. Can you just give me ONE more example?'
Sure. Communication skills.

You'll be surprised by how many people never reach their full potential because they come off as rude.
I saw it as an engineer.

Brilliant engineers who knew a system inside and out would work for subpar engineers who had a way with words.

For this type of leverage to work, you need to have some substance.

If you are solely sweet talking & have 0 technique, then eventually people will find out you're full of shit.

But a grasp of technical knowledge + strong communication skills = **Leverage**.

Overall, it's not about working hard or working smart. When looking closely, the 2 have connections.

Work hard before you can work smart.

Working hard allows accumulates data (experiences).
Working smart allows eliminates wasted movements and zones in on a few things (the old timer playing a pickup game).

It's all connected.

When sticking with a field long term, leverage opportunities begin to emerge over time.

Dennis was a great guy. But in his mind, it was too late for changes to happen with anything regarding technology. I don't know if Dennis still works in the company or not.

However, I know that being stubborn with technology in an engineering industry will be costly over time.

Leverage mixed with consistency propels **'he is going places'** to **'how the hell did he get there??'**

It's a flash which took years to work up to.

What is Awareness?

Awareness is one of the words that are difficult to describe. When you try describing it, it often leaves other people confused.

Awareness is one of those words that you need to **experience**.

I remember a year in a half ago when I had an 'Aha' moment.

I was starting a podcast around that time and decided that I was going to take my practicing more seriously. One of my friends told me I had a lot of work to do. So took the feedback to heart.

For weeks on end, I would practice the podcasting anywhere. In front of a mirror, while driving, walking etc. I'd think of random topics and talk about it. While speaking about it, I would fix up my delivery.

There were days I was thinking with my head & delivering with the heart.

Kept on correcting myself over and over.

One day, as I was about to go to sleep, I had this very sudden realization!

Who the hell was correcting my moves?

I mean, I was using my mind to think of topics & deliver it. But there was this other force that was observing the moves, making notes of what I did right, and what I could improve.

'That sentence was flat, try it again.'

Who is this observer? And why am I JUST noticing it now?

That's when I realized it wasn't my first time noticing it.

It's always been there.

Even when I meditate, there is this force that tells me that I have gotten lost in thought & to bring my focus back to the breath.

I didn't make much of it. But if my mind is thinking, then who is correcting?

That's when I realized that awareness is a force that is meant to be experienced rather than strictly defined.

Still though...

People are naturally curious creatures. There are tons of strange & confusing definitions of awareness. These definitions leave you with more questions than answers.

My favorite discussion into the concept of awareness was from the Bhagavad Gita.

This is where I heard of Samkhya philosophy.

The book brings up the concept of the **Field** and the **Knower**.

The field consists of the mind & matter.

In a lot of scientific studies, the mind & matter are seen as 2 distinct concepts. In the Samkhya philosophy, it is categorized under the same boat.

The field is a flux of energy that changes.
It is the nature of the field to change.

The Knower is the awareness.
It is the observer that is our immortal side.

It does not change. Instead, it is an intelligent force that observes the data of the field.

Anxiety is caused when we identify with the field rather than the Knower.

It is the nature of the mind & body to change. You probably noticed it yourself.

In the morning, you are a person full of energy that is about to tackle the day! Then the evening comes & you are a lazy sack of shit that is unrecognizable.

From this context, you adopted a whole new personality. This was an extreme example, but you get the point.

That's why I enjoy meditation. It allows you to detach from the field, and start identifying more with the Knower.

The still force that is constantly just observing.

You may notice this force before getting on the public speaking stage too.

Before any speech, there is always that person who asks me 'aren't you nervous?'

No clue how I am supposed to answer that.

But it brings awareness.

Are there thoughts of me failing, forgetting a point, getting
booed of stage?
Yes, there is.

But I don't pay attention to those thoughts. I am just there in
the present moment. When I don't give those thoughts much
attention, they begin to disappear.

Am I nervous?
Nope, just aware.

Communication skills is a game of awareness.

A lot of experts get you too caught up with the external world.

Stand like this.
Raise your voice like that.
Wear this.

'Are you saying that's not important?'
Nah, those are important. But all those are secondary.

The primary is focusing on fixing up your internal world.

Communication skills is a derivative of mindset. Sort of like
how orange juice is a derivative of an orange.

You probably had many moments when you were just
present & felt a different force. This force is felt in the present
moment when thinking is suspended.
A few examples include laughing, petting an animal or seeing
a cute baby.

Imagine if you can start harnessing that feeling & locking

into it.

The thing is, *you can.*

It's a lifelong practice though. One that you must commit to. A lot of vehicles out there. Meditation is one of the best resources to begin.

Bottom line is that there is an observer that works THROUGH the mind and body.

Which is why awareness is best experienced, rather than described logically.

Why You're Lazy

One of the biggest sins in the information age is to be lazy.

Well, the biggest sin in any age is to be lazy.

In the information age, it hits different.
'What's the main difference?'
The main difference is that we are more well connected than ever.

I once had someone message me & ask me what Toastmasters was.

Not once...
This guy messaged me 5 times in a row seeking an answer.

His message had gone into my 'message request' folder, so I didn't see it for a few days. By the time I saw it, I was baffled.

Here is this individual, ON THE INTERNET, asking someone else the definition for something.

In the information age, there are things as stupid questions.

In any other age, that may have not been the case. But in the information age? It's time to evolve old school concepts.

Bad Question: What is Toastmasters?
Good Question: How was your experience with Toastmasters?

Laziness disgusts me. It gives me strong physical sensations with a negative perception regarding the other individual.

When I used to work in fast food areas like Dunkin Donuts & Subway, my managers were Desi. One guy was Bengali, and the other guy was Indian.

Bengali's and Indian's often run their store with their micromanager hat on.

One of them would always say 'tara tari tara tari' to his workers. Which is translation for 'hurry hurry.'

All the workers got tips too. But we would all get our tips divided at the end of the day, equally.

I thought that was bullshit.

There were a few workers who dragged their feet the whole shift. And they were going to get the same tip as me?

Nah fam...
But yes, that was the case.

To this day, I don't get the whole 'tip high no matter how the service was' concept. I don't believe that at all. Virtue signaling at its finest.

Tip high if the service was good.
Tip low if the service was bad.

The fast-food industry was great experience for me because I had to work with my hands.

Why are people lazy?

People are lazy when they are chasing something that is blurry or something they don't truly want.

-If you make a kid learn a bunch of topics that they don't see being useful in their life, then it will create **blurriness** for them.

-If you make a kid do something just because his peers are doing it, then the kid's **desire** may not be there.

In terms of the guy who asked me a definition for a word, I'd put him on the latter. If he had a **desire** to learn, then he's not asking for definitions.

Lifelong learners search first and ask second. Especially when they have internet access.

Are you lazy?
'Yes, I am. What do I do?'
Simple. You ask yourself: *how bad do I want it?*

We spend our lives doing things we don't like because others are doing it.

More people are starting businesses in the internet age because the internet is meant to empower you.

The internet does not work with the same rules as the physical world.

When things are TOO easy, it's easy to stop seeing value due to the ease of access.
More people are getting lazier because their life is getting

easier.

This is the generation where you can order groceries from online, watch movies at your place, DM rather than network in person etc.

The easiness should be met with a cautious eye. Stripping away tension is a fast way to devolve into a mediocre personality.

One of the greatest life hacks is to unbalance yourself when you are feeling too balanced.

'Can you give me an example?'
I can.

For my YouTube videos, I have a brand-new chair. But I took off the screws on one side.

'What the fuck, why?'
Because I want to condition my body to stay *still* in my videos. If I move too much, the chair makes an awkward creaking sound.

That level of unbalancing is leading me to consciously balance more in my videos. It is fixing my posture after the videos are done.

There is no magic pill to get rid of laziness.
The lazy person just needs to find a way to unbalance themselves.

Clarify the ambiguity.
Chase true desires.

Laziness is a skill set.
A bad one.

Good news?
Work ethic too is a skill set. And anyone can learn, practice &
master it.

Dark Truth of Modern Trends

Times change.

Yet people have the tendency to carry old ways of thinking into a new world. Media is not the same as it was a couple of years back.

This is why media literacy is more important than ever.

When I was a little kid, what CNN, FOX, MSNBC said was law. This was our main method to get news.

In analogy terms, view yourself at a wedding. In the wedding, a set entrée is being served.

Nowadays, CNN, FOX, MSNBC are just one of the many different media platforms out there.

New media is fueled by the internet and new media has turned the landscape of media from an **autocracy to a meritocracy.**

Now view yourself at a wedding. But rather than having a set entrée...
The wedding has a buffet.
You pick and choose.

Plenty missed the memo on the pick & choose part. They are stuck in thinking that only an entrée is being served.

Around 2018, I recall a bunch of people eating Tide Pods. Around 2019, there were people who were opening a tub of ice-cream at a grocery shop, licking the top, recording it & sticking the ice-cream back in the fridge.

Nasty clowns.

Why would people behave like this?
Because others did.

Not understanding that new media works in a brand-new law than traditional media can have people missing out on opportunities while viewing barbaric acts as opportunities.

The stunning realization I recently noticed is the similarity that media is having with the world of physics.

What Traditional media is to New media is what Newtonian physics is to Quantum physics.

Newtonian physics works great with macroscopic objects. The laws work perfectly to make sense of the world.

But when you go small, it seems like the Newtonian laws no longer work. The world of quantum holds different rulesets.

In the world of physics, there too are individuals who are just stuck in their ways.
'This quantum stuff is a fad! It's not real.'

Some quantum physicists may say the same about Newtonian physics.
'Get with the time's already!'

The truth is that both groups are correct. It's just a game of knowing when to apply which.

I am not of the belief that Traditional media is going to be obsolete anytime soon. One day, it may be. But I do believe there's a group for it.

However, we should not project the centralization to the world of new media. Have a "pick & choose buffet" mentality in this world of the internet.

I love when people subscribe.
I love when people unsubscribe.
Choices.

This is surprisingly the golden era of media & very few people are noticing.

To extend the analogy of physics further...
Neil Bohr, a famous quantum physicist said:
"If quantum mechanics hasn't profoundly shocked you, you haven't understood it yet."

The same will be said about the internet as it continues to evolve.

Sharing Your Story

Around 2016, my company sent me to Chicago to meet my team.

You see, my job position was in Tampa. But all my team members worked in Chicago. I was what you called, a **remote employee.**

My Chicago manager was feeling nice. He booked me in an expensive hotel. It was the Trump Hotel.

Around that time, Donald Trump was running for president, and things were getting very tense.

When I landed in Chicago & went to check into my room, I saw a bunch of protestors outside.

As I tried to go past them to enter the building, there was this lady with glasses who angrily asked me:
'How could you possibly support this man? Especially considering your skin color!'

Look lady, my flight already got delayed 3 times. Move out of my way so I can go take a nap.

Well, the next few days were just as busy in front of the hotel. However, it was great meeting the team.

From 9am-5pm, I would work & get training.
For the remaining part of the day, it was all about exploring Chicago.

One day, I am coming back from a long day of work and the front of the hotel is empty. This is strange. No protestors in sight.

That's when I see this man who looks JUST like R Kelly sitting in front of the building smoking a cigar.

His resemblance to R Kelly was crazy. This must've been his doppelganger!

As I was staring at this man, a part of me started to think: *Wait a minute. Is this R Kelly?*

As I am looking at this individual, he is looking back at me. He puts his cigar down & is like:
'What's good young homie?'

Startled that he noticed me, I had to ask:
Not to be rude bro, but are you R Kelly? You look just like him.

He laughed and said:
'Yea man, I am.'

Holy shit, this was so random. This was before his whole trial and everything.

He was still involved in controversy. Not condoning all that. But in 2016, I wasn't aware of any of that news.

All I was aware of was how 'ignition' would come on in my bus & we would all go wild.

Asked him if I could take a picture.
He said yes.

Didn't want to waste too much of his time. So just asked him 1
final question:
*Yo, how have you stayed consistent with your music for so
long?*

His response was surprising. He said:
'I don't write music. I talk about life in song format.'

That was a major PARADIGM shift.

This was before I was involved in ArmaniTalks.
Yet, this insight came in clutch for my job at the time.

The problem being a remote employee in Tampa with a team
in Chicago was the communication.

I felt very stiff communicating with these people.
- o   *Felt like I had to write an email.*
- o   *I had to write a chat message.*

Everything felt robotic.

When my co-workers in Chicago finally met me, they got to
see my personality. But how can I do that when I go back to
Tampa?

It's a game of just talking about life.
**Have a conversation in email form, rather than writing an
email.**
This connects to the human side, rather than the machine.
In terms of telling a story, it comes down to

talking about life.

Nothing more complicated is needed.
Especially when you are telling 'your story.'

I've never liked elevator pitches. And say I'm a person of power, never would I want to hear an elevator pitch. Rather, I would just want to see that the person is engaged in the project that they are working on.

A few years after that Chicago trip, I ended up getting a manager in Tampa. And he was this *tell it like it is* guy from New York. He had that New York *'in your face'* vibe to him.

His name was Ed.

Ed would blatantly say:
'I hate all that fancy lingo. The more people talk all that shit, the more nervous they are...or they don't know what the fuck they are talking about.'

This is a man of power in the company cursing away.
However, it was giving a lot of insights into human behavior.

Doing monotonous work on a daily routine has us getting away from the human side in communication.

However, the more that we rise in a field, the more we have to realize that all these technologies that's being generated...
When you get to the essence of it all:
It's comes down to making it easier to communicate.

We aim to make our lives easier so we can focus

on the stuff that matters.

It just keeps coming down to that. Check out most technology in your house right now. You'll find a way to connect it to humans in some way.

So don't try to 'tell a story.'
Talk about life in story format.

Don't try to write an email.
Have a conversation in email format.

Don't see how to grow your followers.
Give value & see how the right people can find you.

Have the technology morph around your voice.
Not the other way around. That's how we tell our story in this ever-changing world.

What Made Seinfeld Successful

I want to talk about 2 things:
-Seinfeld, the show.
-Seinfeld, the person.

What made him successful?

The show Seinfeld is seen as the "show about nothing."

A show about nothing?? No way is something like this going to be successful.

False. A show about nothing has the recipe to be extremely successful.
Why?

I can't say the exact reason why. But I have a theory.

Normally, there is a certain segment in my day where I don't like thinking at all. And my disdain towards thinking (at that time) has me missing old school media.

In old school TV programming, I had a channel called the TV guide. That channel showed what was being played on TV at the time. I saw what show/movie was being played on what channel & chose that.

If I was too lazy to go to the TV guide, then I would just aimlessly channel surf until I saw something that I liked.

This is different in new media.

Cable cutting is at an all-time high. Nowadays, most people consume their shows through Netflix or YouTube. Plenty of choices!

This can be a good thing or a bad thing.
Depending on the state of mind that you are in.

If I'm in the state of mind where I'm not trying to think, the last thing I want is plenty of choices.

I miss it when the traditional media was like, 'here's what is showing. Take it or leave it.'
They took the power.

Well, this little psychology insight was what allowed Seinfeld to be successful. You didn't necessarily have to think too much. You could just unwind & watch. This chill factor led to constant exposure of the show.

With our best friends, are we mindful or mindless?

'I can be either. I like my friends a lot because I can be mindless around them without anyone taking offense.'
Exactly.

The show Seinfeld could serve as a friend. That one friend who won't get offended if you hypothetically were not paying attention to something they said, because they knew you had a long day.

A show about nothing can be highly appealing to a segment of the population.

The next question:
What made Jerry Seinfeld, the person, successful?

I'm going to give an obvious answer & then I'm going to give a not so obvious answer.

The obvious answer is that he was consistent. He would write every day. He took his field of comedy very seriously & made it his life.

What's not obvious is that he was a little awkward. Specifically, in social interactions.

'What do you mean?'
He said in an interview a while back that he finds it difficult to relate to people in normal ways of communication.

Small talk, gossip, talking on the phone, that kind of stuff.

On the contrary, he finds it easy to relate to people through his career.
Comedy.

Something about a comedian feels highly personal. It's like we are letting them into our world.

Well, Jerry noticed that. He said comedy was his vehicle to maintain relationships in an unorthodox manner.

I did notice this about highly creative people.
The more creative they are, the more one or plenty parts of their lives are very unorthodox.
They do things differently.

Different is good for some.
Different is bad for some.

Depends on which lens we view it from.

Overall, these were a few things that made Seinfeld successful. The show & the person.

There's no denying that Seinfeld showed that it's normal to be weird & weird to be normal.

The Secret Language of your Brain

Around April 2019th, I decided to invest more time into YouTube. I'm not a professional camera guy or anything, but figured I'd learn along the way.

My mom & friend gave me an idea to turn my apartment into a studio. So, I decided to do it. Much better than looking for a new location every video.

As I began creating the new studio, I was going through a lot of trial & errors. I kept readjusting stuff & trying to make it look nice.

But each time, *I fell short.*

It seemed like a lot of work. I knew I wanted the studio to look a certain way but kept screwing it up.

After a bunch of trials, I realized the mistake I was making. I realized I was trying to create this studio without having a picture in mind. I was just winging it.

This was a problem because I didn't give my mind something to work towards. Which caused me to spin in circles.

Luckily this error pointed me in the right direction. I randomly started to go into some thought experiments.

When we move our furniture, what do we do?
We picture the end goal first, then we begin moving the

furniture items. When it doesn't look the way we wanted it to, we picture something else & reconfigure.

This insight allowed me to make a mini studio.

I took some time to visualize a rough look of what the setup should look like. Even did a bit of doodling to guide the visualization process.

The lesson was that the brain needs specificity. And it will get that specificity through a **picture**.

'So Armani, if I want to become a great public speaker, are you saying I need to picture myself being a great public speaker?'
Correct. It's tough, but doable.

If I were to tell you to picture a Coca Cola bottle with wings on it, you would surprisingly be able to do it.
'I see it.'

Try seeing a pink cow.
'Wow, I see that too.'

What about a black giraffe?
'Oh my, I see that too!!'

But how are you seeing these images? They aren't real.

Doesn't matter. Your imagination doesn't care. Your imagination will see what you tell it to see.

Drawing, writing, whatever.
Learn the art of crystallizing.

Making it realistic never hurts. You can write out that you want to see yourself with wings, but you aren't getting wings!

On the flipside, you don't have to be too realistic. Grand dreams are killed because grand dreams were never envisioned.

It may seem crazy to the logical mind that you will one day be speaking in front of 500 people with ease.

The logical mind will be like:
'But you can barely speak in front of 5 people with ease! How can you speak in front of 500 people? Be realistic!'

This example is much different than the example with you envisioning yourself with wings. Can you tell me why?

'I think I know but tell me.'
It's because you are physically capable.

Whenever you are physically capable of something, now the ball is in the mind's court.
Now the narrative is based on work ethic, drive & commitment.

Just need to work your way up to specificity champ.

An input in writing format can cause your imagination to output a picture image.
Powerful stuff.

When you understand what I am saying you'll grasp the secret language of the brain.

Pictures...

The Art of Patience

The year was 2017 & I needed to get an oil change. This was going to be a problem.

'Why?'
Because I had always gone to my usual spot to get an oil change. But this year, I had just moved & I had to find a new 'usual spot.'

I'll be honest. I don't know much about cars & often don't know when I'm getting ripped off. And every time I took my car to the shop, they would try to up sell me on 30 other things. But things were different with Luke.

'Who the fuck is Luke?'
Luke was the last guy who would take care of my car when I needed to get the oil changed. He was an honest guy who wouldn't try to up sell me for no reason.

Anyways Armani, quit bitchin. Find someone new.

I did some research & saw the closest thing was a Firestone. Eh, I hate the corporations. But everything else was a good distance away.

Firestone, it is.

I end up going to Firestone & see a LONG line. Ah damn, it's going to be a long day.

After waiting in line for 20 minutes, I finally am the next to be served. It's a 35-year-old gentleman, sloppy hair & looks slow with his movements.

He asked me what I needed & I told him about the oil change. He gave me some paperwork & told me he'd have a mechanic look at it.

I went to a chair, filled out the paperwork & gave it to him. He said thanks & said they are beginning my oil change.

That's it? I thought.
No up sell??

Yes! That was it. No up sell. It's not going to be as bad as I thought.

So, I end up going back to the waiting area & now finding a way to kill time. I was on my phone watching YouTube videos until I saw my phone was at 1%.

Shit.... Aight, I'll just watch TV that they have playing.

I spent the next hour watching CNN.

Holy shit, this is brutal....

After an hour had passed, I was getting a little annoyed. What's taking so long? It's just a simple oil change. And I can't watch CNN any longer!

I decide to pick up a magazine with Odell Beckham Jr in the front and began reading it.

2 more hours had passed on by. I finished the magazine.

At this point, I was getting agitated as fuck. 3 hours for an oil change?? Come on man..

So, I go up & I see another massive line has formed. Damn.

I wait in the line for 30 more minutes & see the same guy at the counter again.

'Yes, how can I help you sir?' he says.
Hello. Been here for a while. Any update on the oil change?
'We are working on it sir' he said in a disgruntled voice.
Aight bro.

I sat back down. Now it was either watch CNN or read a magazine on Gardening.

Damn man, I knew Luke wouldn't pull something like this.

Another hour in a half passes on by. At this point, I am pissed!!!

Practically 4 hours of my life just sitting & doing nothing??? There's no way I'm paying for this shit.

I go up again & this time there's another man sitting on the counter. Ah great, now I have to explain what's going on to this new guy.

'Hello sir, how can I help you?' the new guy said enthusiastically.

I was a little irritated by the enthusiasm in his voice considering what I was going thru. But I explained the story anyways.

'Whoa, 4 plus hours?? No way. Let me figure out what's going on!' said the new guy.

He goes to the mechanic workshop area & begins talking to some people. And he comes back looking very grim.

Any update?? I ask.
'Um sir... I'm very sorry. But unfortunately, the mechanics forgot to begin on your car' he said with sadness.

Forgot?? I asked in confusion.
'Yes sir. The whole oil change will be on the house & I am so sorry for the inconvenience & miscommunication.'

I kid you not, I wanted to yell at this guy. Even though it wasn't his fault, I needed **someone** to be mad at.

Wanted to let him know how unprofessional this was, how I was going to give this place a bad review & how they lost my business forever.

But something happened.
'What?'
I decided not to...

'How come you didn't get mad at him?'
No clue. I just said, 'thanks for the update' and went back to my seat and waited.

20 minutes later, they had my car ready & offered me 2 free oil changes for the next time.

The gentleman in the counter said sorry multiple amounts of times & couldn't thank me enough for my patience. He truly did appreciate it.

That moment really changed my life in many ways.

I still have no clue why I didn't snap at him. Growing up, I had a noticeably short temper. But something different happened that day.

Rather than leading with my ego, I led with the heart.

You'll also be put in situations like this. A situation where you have all the reasons in the world to get angry.

Nah, scratch that.
All the reasons in the world to get **livid**.

And you'll have 2 options:
-Option 1. Let your emotions overpower your mind.
-Option 2. Let your mind overpower your emotions.

Whichever route you choose, will be the behavior that you reinforce for future scenarios like this.

I kid you not...

But patience is one of the most important traits in the real world. ESPECIALLY when you are competent.

When you are competent in your profession or just have your shit together, it's VERY easy to be impatient.

'Why do you say that?'
Because you'll see how many people are not professional & do not have their shit together.

Old school me was a perfectionist & wanted others to be the same. When they did not live up to my ego, I got mad.

Nowadays, I lead with the heart in social interactions.

I accept that humans are flawed creatures & they are going to make mistakes.

They are rarely making the mistake on purpose to harm you. I don't think the mechanics in the shop had a vendetta against me or anything. I think it was a busy day at the shop & they forgot about my car.

And snapping at the new dude who had nothing to do with it would have been very socially unintelligent on my end.

When you take the road less taken & maintain your patience, you feel immensely proud of yourself. I felt very proud after maintaining my cool that day.

On the contrary, when you are impatient & lose your cool, you feel like the 'boss' at first. But once time elapses, you feel a lot of shame.

The best tip to maintain patience is to think LONG term, not short term. You will feel VERY uncomfortable as you are being patient. But ultimately, you will thank yourself later for it.

The skin will toughen.

And your composure will battle test you for other rocky situations that the real world presents.

Maintain patience, even when it seems like the hardest thing to do.

Patience is a staple of the world of communications. It takes you from being impulsive to calculated. And luckily, it is a skill set that can be developed.

The Yin & Yang of Communication Skills

In the communications world, a lot of things don't make sense. To illustrate this point, think about your closest friend.

The friend that you have known through multiple stages of your life. Got it?
'Yes.'

Now imagine the first time meeting this friend. If you don't remember how y'all met, then think about the beginning stages of the relationship.

In the beginning stages, you two barely knew each other. There were some surface level conversations, but that was about it.

But you two continued the relationship. The both of you met up more times & began to strengthen the bond.

As the bond grew, you guys started developing inside jokes, hanging out with each other more & talked about future goals. All that stuff.

Now here's where things get interesting. At this point, a lot of the emotions have been *positive*.

An argument here or there, but nothing too serious.

However, at this point, there is a fork in the road. This is where a difference between a friend & a **best** friend is born.

A best friend is often born through darkness. You two had each other's back during a *very* dark moment. Showing loyalty despite bad circumstances strengthened the bond. It connected the two of you on a deeper level.

The friendship started off in the light.
But it was solidified in the dark.
That is the Yin & Yang of communication skills.

In a logical world, something like this doesn't make much sense. But in the social world, it makes all the sense in the world.

What does this mean?

It means making someone feel multiple emotions solidifies the bond quicker.

You ever seen that one person keep going back to a toxic ex? 'Too many times to count. Why was that?'
It's because they have both felt a spectrum of emotions with one another.

Happy, angry, sad, happy again, confused & so much more. It glued them together.

The opposite is true as well.

The worst thing to do for a social bond is to detach. That's when you aren't making them feel any emotion from the emotional spectrum.

Sometimes detachment is intentional. Let's say you are trying to cut off a person because this person did you wrong. Then detachment is a clear indicator that the social bond is willingly being destroyed in real time.

Other times, detachment is unintentional.
Aka: a boring personality.

In the social world, being boring is a sin.
A person becomes boring when they don't make their conversation partner feel any form of emotions.

In the public speaking world, the Yin & Yang formula is relevant as well. I call it negative visualization.

Picture a negative thing happening in your speech & then picture yourself overcoming it.

Negative & positive.

No matter where the eyes are laid upon in the social world, dual energies exist.

Personalizing the duality causes stress, anxiety & rage.

Viewing the dual energies as play gives an alternate approach to life.
- o We laugh in movies.
- o We cry in movies.

Why stop with movies?

All of life is one large story. One large play where energies are being exchanged in utter harmony.

How to Work with Intent

You ever had that moment when you work hard at something, but weren't sure why?

Yea, you have.

The perfect example is networking.

When I first got into the work force, my managers told me about the importance of networking. Said it was something that I should invest in if I wanted to get ahead. So, I would go to a bunch of networking events & talk.

At first, it seemed all fine. But after attending a few networking events, I realized I **hated** it.

All the fake smiles, small talk & conversations about stuff that I didn't care about. I didn't like it at all. Felt painful to be honest.

Eventually, I would skip out on networking events & just head home after work. I felt like my time was much better spent that way.

A few years went by & I realize why I hated networking.

It was because I had no clue why I was doing it.

I mean sure, I heard the phrase 'you'll get ahead.' But to be frank, I wasn't too sure what that meant at the time.

I was working without intent.

Without intent, the smallest roadblocks seem like massive hurdles.

On the contrary, with intent, the massive hurdles will seem like small roadblocks.

'How do I work with intent?'
Honest truth? Working with intent is earned.

You'll never fully work with intent when you are beginning something.

I mean you will in the first phase, when you're filed with emotion. But after a while of taking losses, you will want to quit.

(Picture the people who make New Year's Resolutions in the beginning of the year & quit due to the pain of working out/dieting).

Same scenario with networking.

I was filled with enthusiasm to 'get ahead' in the beginning of my journey.

But after a handful of boring conversations, I wanted to quit.

Persevering through this phase will dictate whether you work with intent or not.

You see, the painful phase will help you decide whether you want it or not. However, you need to go PAST the painful phase to make that conclusion.

All too often, we quit during the pain.

When you go past the painful phase, the conscious act will become a subconscious one. You will also have seen exactly what not to do to build a refined focus on what to do.

At that stage, intent is unlocked. The very messy act is now crystal clear.

'Is finding the intent always painful? Can it be painless?' Sure. Learn from other people's mistakes (this is why listening is so important).

I had a friend who had gotten addicted to social media a few years back. And when I had gotten into social media, he warned me about his pitfall.

So, I learned & now my intent on social media is to either network, learn or produce. Not bullshit around. I didn't make the same mistake as him because he taught me the intent.

Intent is huge for communication as well. The ones who don't have intent talk in circles or say something in a cowardly fashion. Every leader out there has intent behind their words.

No need to agree with their opinions but can't deny that the energy is felt.

Without intent, there will always be an invisible ceiling holding you back from taking it to the next level.

Shatter that ceiling and fly towards greatness.

How to Be Mentally RICH

Have you ever noticed yourself going through those bouts of self-doubt, negative thoughts & defeat?

We all have. That's just comes with the territory of the human mind.

Luckily, there is a way around this. There is a framework that successful people follow to always keep on executing.

You may think that the successful person does not feel doubt.

But they do...

And they feel a ton of it because they are always growing & entering new ventures that they are not well-versed in.

I still feel the same exact nerves I did when I was first beginning public speaking all the way up until now. 500 people or 5 people, it doesn't matter. The nerves are always there.

So, what keeps these people going you wonder?

It's a simple insight:
Thoughts are not reality.

When you can make this realization, your paradigm begins to shift.

When you realize thoughts are simply illusions of reality,

then you get to decide which thoughts to give weight to &
which not to.

Imagine I came up to you with 2 other people. Mary & Jake.

Then I told you that if you could spot which one was telling
the truth & which one wasn't, I'd give you 50 dollars. You
eagerly accept.

Mary says: 'You are a human.'
Jake says: 'You are an alien.'

Well, who told the truth?
'Mary, duh!!'
What makes you say that? They both used words.
'Yea, but Jake used words that were CLEARLY not true.'
Exactly.

Just because you have certain thoughts does not mean that
it's true. In many cases, it's not!

But you will not be able to tell which thoughts are true
& which aren't if you have no clue who you are & who you
want to be.

The bottom line is that thoughts are *only as real as you make
them.*

This is exactly why you should be meditating. Spend 5
minutes doing it & see random stuff that do and don't make
sense.

That is what successful people understand. They
understand that all thoughts aren't reality.

But here's one more bonus tip:
**They know they will predominately think the thoughts that
they consume.**

 Life Laws:
-You are what you eat.
-You become what you consume.

Winners aren't watching the garbage on mainstream media,
fight videos & reality tv nonstop. It's because the brain is
being programmed to think MORE negative thoughts.

Even though the winner knows that thoughts aren't real, the
act of thinking an abundance of negative thoughts becomes
burdensome.

Keep consuming content that leaves you feeling enlightened
& like a winner. You can do this through books, videos &
podcasts.

*-The more you feed your mind wealth, the RICHER your
thoughts become.*

*-The richer your thoughts become, the more valuable YOU
become.*

The law of the universe rewards a valuable human.

Thoughts aren't real. But empowering thoughts never hurt.

Heck, it will be the difference between mediocrity & a life full
of abundance.

Attraction Networking

Networking is never easy at first. Especially when it seems like everyone else knows each other, while you are left standing on the sidelines.

I used to be 'that guy.'

You know, that guy who stands on the side hoping for someone to start a conversation with them. Or that guy who is circling the networking event with those creepy googly eyes.

That was me.

When I moved to Virginia for a brief period, I knew things were going to get bumpy.

By the time I landed in this new location, I realized I needed to make some friends. So, I began attending Meetup events.

'How was it?'
Awkward!
'Why was it awkward?'
Because it seemed like everyone knew each other & I was some alien.

I remember for my first Meetup event, I was standing on the side for a long time before I realized that I **needed** to break the ice with someone. Everyone was in groups.

So, I walk up to a group of 5 people where 1 guy is telling a story. And for some reason, I blurt out 'Whatsup guys! I'm

Armani.'

The guy telling the story was visibly upset after being cut
off *(I think he was about to get to the good part)*. But he
allowed me to join the group anyways.

The group tried creating conversation with me & vice versa.
But it just felt extremely uncomfortable. One forced sentence
after another.

1 hour later after hopping from group to group, I felt drained.

I went home that day & decided that networking was
overrated. Realized that was the last time I was entering a
networking event again!!

But wait.

Then I realized that I was someone new to town. I didn't have
many options you know.

Networking was pretty much my **only** option to make friends.
I decided to suck it up & keep showing face.

For the next few months, I began to attend event after event.
And something began to change.

'What?'
I was no longer that guy who no one knew.

Eventually, after showing my face a bunch of times, & having
mini conversations, I was starting to become known.

Now, many different groups knew who I was. They would
often invite me over, or I'd create a group by myself.

I'd keep an extra eye out for guests, so they didn't have to go through the awkwardness like I did.

Soon, every event I went to, I had new people coming up to me. Having a group to talk to made me much more approachable than the guy gawking at others from the side.

Why do I tell you this?

I reached the attraction networking stage AFTER putting in the work.

When you enter a brand-new networking event, it's going to feel uncomfortable at first. You don't know anyone.

It's easy to let that initial awkwardness rule out going to another one of those events again.

Big mistake. Because everyone you know was a stranger at one point or another.

Networking feels awkward because you begin off at the uncomfortable stage at scale. It feels like the whole world is watching you.

Nah homie. They are all focused on themselves. Just keep being social.

Event after event of showing face, familiarity builds. The networking muscle gets stronger & it begins to feel easier to talk to others.

Soon, you'll begin to **magnetize** others.

Now, this is one way to go about it. Another way to do attraction networking is via social media.

Be one of those accounts who always provides value in one way or another.

Don't be the loser who goes on social media & whines all the time.

Rather, provide value by entertaining, educating and/or sharing some wisdom. This route requires you to invest in yourself, share your message via your content & attract winners.

I recommend having a level of offline & online presence.

The offline presence will require you to fight through the initial discomfort, keep showing up to events, build familiarity & have others come up to you.

The online presence will require you to set up your social profiles, keep providing value & have others contact you.

Either way, it's a win-win.

Life is a game of people. Those who play the game stack up opportunities while those who opt out of the game twiddle their thumbs missing out on opportunities.

The Lifelong Student

Within a few weeks into being a member of Toastmasters, I knew that the club was highly slept on.

Too underrated!

It felt like a hand full of meetings in the club caused me to warp my personality in real time.

Toastmasters gave me enhanced social skills, public speaking, the ability to communicate with different cultures...

And confidence.

After a few meetings, some of my friends began noticing changes in me. They would pull me aside at times to ask if the club could help them.

'Why'd they pull you aside?'
Because they didn't want others knowing they struggled with public speaking.

I let them know the club can help them. It's great for people who want to overcome speech anxiety. So, they came to a few meetings with me.

However, there was this one guy, who would always say, 'I don't need Toastmasters.'

He was a very well-spoken guy in 1 on 1 conversations. But I never saw him talking in front of a scaled audience.

I asked him what made him so confident in his public

speaking?

He said, *'I had to give class presentations during college.'*

This was small time thinking in my world. He thinks public speaking ends in the classroom. But that was it for his progress, I guess.

After I started ArmaniTalks, I have worked with many clients from different fields. Some real estate investors, entrepreneurs & a few doctors.

The unique part?

Most were much older than me.
They were in their 40s-50s.

Successful individuals who were willing to learn from someone younger. They never bought up my age. They were just after insights into the skill set.

Each of us has our own skillsets that we are a few steps ahead of someone else on.

That's why the lifelong student is always steps ahead even when they are steps behind someone.

They keep their mind open.

The open mind is what allows you to level up. Gaining practical insights is key.

I've learned from individuals much younger than me. Nowadays, I don't even see age. I just see if they have some skin in the game or not.

Lifelong students always get smarter.

The mind needs something to do. It's the nature of the mind to *move*. When you close it off, it starts spinning in circles, causing anxiety.

The goal is to direct the mind. Make it one pointed on a task.

Sort of like when you're driving. Its best to decide where you are going to go eat, then get in your car. Failing to decide the destination will have you driving all over the place.

KFC, McDonalds, Chinese???

Lifelong students have general knowledge built around specialized interests.

Specialized interests are stuff they are naturally curious about. Those are the core topics of their curriculum.

Then they are led to a lot of different areas of study that relate to the core in one way or another.

For example:
Say you are genuinely interested in public speaking.

If you decide to study it, somehow, you'll also brush along psychology, emotional intelligence, storytelling, creativity etc.

Whatever you do, don't close your mind off. Keep learning. If it's the nature of the mind to move, might as well put it to some good use.

When Keeping It Real Goes Wrong

In 2014, it was me, 3 friends & this random kid driving to a funeral. A sad occasion to say the least.

All the passengers in the car were noticeably quiet & in a somber mood.

Eventually, a few hours had passed & we had a few more hours to go until we got to the destination.

Around that point, the driver decided to get slick.

He knew me & the other passenger in the car would normally clown each other. So, the driver decided to start some random roast off.

The driver says, 'yo Armani, a few weeks ago Billy (the other guy) said your shorts looked whack.'

Billy woke up from his mild nap and nodded his head. 'Yea bro, your shorts were whack as fuck. Where did you get it from, Ross?'
The whole car started laughing.

I was not in the mood to roast back.
But me & Billy had history.

For some reason, we always had this strange tension between us. Both of us were friends, yes.

But at times, we questioned this.

I said nothing back.

Billy went on roasting my outfit even more and the car continued to laugh.

Eventually, I had enough & I started roasting back. Billy's hair was thinning.

Anytime you made fun of his pushed back hairline, his face would turn red.

Once I started firing back, the roast-off was on.

As we were roasting each other, I noticed something annoying.
'What?'
Raul.

There was this random kid who I never met in my life in the car with us. He was the driver's friend, but I wasn't cool with him like that.

Raul kept taking Billy's side & making me look like a fool. 'That's all you got Armani? That's corny!' Raul would say.

I was getting annoyed with Raul. Just pipe down and watch from afar. I don't even know you like that. Him hyping up Billy was making me look like the losing side.

It got to a point where the roast off was turning heated. *Not only a LITTLE heated.* But we were dropping some serious bombs.

We were getting personal.

Billy kept calling me an electrician. I have nothing against electricians, but I was a trained *electrical engineer.*

Calling an electrical engineer an electrician seems like a slight jab, but in the fraternity of engineers, we don't appreciate the mix-up.

I then blurted out, 'well, this electrician makes double what you make!'
That's when the whole car got quiet.

I saw Billy & he looked sad.
Looked like he was going to cry.

Even the people in the car who were neutral were like, 'Come on Armani. That's below the belt.'

I didn't know this was below the belt.
Actually, scratch that. I did.

This was a bad moment for me because Billy and I always had a strange relationship. But we trusted each other to a certain degree.

I don't normally like telling others how much I make. Posting screenshots of how deep my pockets are was never my style. It wasn't Billy's style either.

Yet we trusted each other enough to disclose how much we made in our jobs. And in this roast battle, I took advantage of that information.

The rest of the car ride was quiet.

We attended the funeral...
And the rest of the car ride back was just as quiet.

This was a great example of when keeping it real goes wrong.

When jokes are weaponized.

The cool thing about guys is that we often forgive & forget quick. That is how it was like with Billy.

The apology went with me saying 'Yo bro, my bad for the car ride the other day.'
His response 'all good man.'

Boom, back to normal.

Still, the silence in the car ride after I made that comment still sticks with me to this day.
Since then, I realized that words do have power.

In today's world, more humans are thin skinned. Remember this. Just because you are thick skinned does not mean others are like you.

Always assume others are more sensitive than you think, so your words are more tactical & your tonality is more soothing.

The whole sticks & stones may break my bones, but names will never hurt me only works with a rare few.

And even a thick-skinned person has something that he or she is VERY sensitive towards.

Like a hard ass marine who gets angry when you make fun of him for marrying his cheating ex-wife.

Keeping it real goes wrong when you assume words are just words. Words are more than that.

Words have the power to build or to destruct.
Jokes are all good & fun. But there is always a fine line.

At times, we may inadvertently cross that fine line. When that happens, just sack up & apologize champ.

Winners apologize when they are wrong & losers get creative on why they were not wrong...

Is Twitter Worth It?

Twitter was one of those apps that I was not sold on before.
My first experience with Twitter was comical.

I knew this kid James who considered himself this 'macho'
guy. He would always try to prove how tough he was.

He'd say stuff like:
-*Boneless wings are for bitches.*
-*If you don't drink beer, then you're a pussy.*
-*Real men only watch football, not any other sports.*

James felt like a cartoon character, but he provided me good
laughs.

During my undergrad year, I saw him one day giggling on
his phone in the library.

The first time I heard him, I let it slide. The second & third
time I heard him, he caught my curiosity.

Yo, what you laughing at? I asked.
'One of the football players I follow tweeted something funny
haha' he responded.

At that time, Facebook was popping. I had NO clue what
Twitter was. So, I asked him about it.

He was talking about how it's a platform where you can
follow your favorite celebrities and interact with them.

James said that Twitter would be the future.

Around that time, there was another guy in the table named Paul, who busted out laughing.

'Here you are always claiming manhood and you are following a bunch of men like a cheerleader. YOU are the wimp.' Paul said jokingly.

Paul was waiting to get that off his chest. Especially since James would not stop making fun of him for getting a light blue car.

Overall, the conversation was funny. I thought Paul had a point. Why the hell would I want to follow a bunch of celebrities? Seems weird.

As time has gone on, my thoughts on Twitter have evolved.

Nowadays, I don't see it as a platform for mindless consumption.

I see it as a platform for mindful creation & consumption.

Twitter is different because it requires the consumer to READ. When you read, you make your brain work. Even if it's just a little.

There's a big difference between watching a fiction movie & reading a fiction book.

-For a fiction movie, all the scenes are presented to you.
-For a fiction book, you ACTIVELY must use your brain to turn words into out of world images.

The latter is a stronger workout.

I used to run Instagram pages. One of my most popular pages was for extreme sports. I built a whole community around it.

I loved my time on Instagram. Could never see another app overtaking it. Especially one like Twitter.

However, as time has elapsed, Twitter & YouTube are my favorites.
I believe it allows for the richest content consumption when used strategically.

Now with all that being said, is Twitter worth it?
Well, it would be smart to define what 'worth it' means.

My brand is all about building confidence through communication. In my eyes, yes, it is worth it.

Twitter allows me to test ideas that I can use for speeches, YouTube videos, and conversation material.

The low number of characters for each tweet forces me to actively turn thoughts into words and be succinct in the process.

People who tweet a lot speak clearer and get to the point quicker.

To build a business, Twitter has been worth it.
It's a creator to consumer model. No funny business with all these middlemen.

Twitter has been a great journey for me. I believe anyone who wants to improve their communication skills with the lowest risk should invest in a Twitter.

If you don't want to show your face, then be anonymous. If you want to show your face, then post up a nice picture of yourself, just so you take the account seriously.

Not a grainy pic with your dog licking on your forehead.

There are so many people that use the app for a bunch of nonsense. Using it as a diary to bitch out loud.

Imagine how pathetic that must feel. Displaying why you're a victim so others can feel sorry for you. That could never be me.

'What should I tweet about?'
That's only a question you can answer.

For me, it started off with sharing my public speaking journey with Toastmasters. But it evolved to talking about social skills, building a brand, writing a book & my life philosophy.

Twitter is an entity that grows with you.

Writing is powerful & can be a very enjoyable hobby.

If I could redo one thing over again, I'd have begun writing earlier.

Oh well, June 18, 2018, my first tweet went up.
And I'm just getting started. I hope to see you join me for the ride.

Dangers Of Being Too Humble

Being humble to a certain extent is great. It allows you to maintain creativity without coming off like an ass.

No one likes the person who always brags.
It's annoying.

However, being too humble is almost as bad as bragging too much.

Too much of anything is dangerous in this world.

I used to have a graphic designer who would create cover photos on a website that I used to own. She was gifted.

Every now and then I would get her on a call to just make sure she was clear about the job posting. She had a soft voice.

She would always respond with 'yes yes...'
In a soft, hurried way.

Rarely would ask questions.

In the beginning, this would worry me because I thought she hadn't understood the full job posting and would miss the mark.

But each time, I was wrong.

Each time, she delivered with flying colors.
The quality given was **much** more than the quantity paid.

It came to a point where I was curious what else she could do. I mean she's so good at graphic design... Can she, I don't know.....maintain the website too?

The answer was, yes. She was also a webmaster as well. This girl was a WordPress pro.

After working more with her, I found out she could also do video editing as well. A huge powerhouse!

'What's the point of all this Armani? Just seems like you found a great worker.'
Not quite. The lesson is a little deeper.

I found out about her talents due to **active prying on my end**.

She was not letting me know. I'm sure even by the time we stopped working together, I only discovered 10% of what she was capable of.

It's sad how such a talented person holds back their powers. Her business was built around her too.

One day, I asked her why she held back?
Her response was *hehe, I don't want to brag too much.'*

The intent is correct.
Yet, the method is wrong.

What's funny about this whole thing was that I had a

webmaster before her. And the dude sucked! Always fucking shit up.

But what he did have was confidence.
He was his biggest hype man.

'Armani, I have been doing WordPress for __many years and I have worked with clients like blah blah blah.'
I believed it.

In a world where you invest in yourself, the next step up is marketing yourself.

If you don't market yourself, then people who DIDN'T invest in themselves will gladly do so.

Pretty funny when you think about it. But it's more sad when you really look into it.

Being humble has a place in this world. But being too humble takes away your opportunities.

If you know you're skilled & there is a pain point to be met, then go on and offer the solution.

My paradigm flipped last year when someone said they read Level Up Mentality (my first published book) while they were having suicidal thoughts. And the book helped them turn their life around.

Since then, I heard more comments about the book. Which I personally found to be powerful.

If I wrote the book, and never put it on Gumroad or Amazon,

then it would be good as useless.

It would benefit me because I got writing experience. But the POTENTIAL is not being met.

Building your skills is level 1. But you always gotta' eventually level up to letting it be known.

The beauty is that the more you practice your skills, the more you feel confident overcoming the impostor syndrome. We don't want to promote ourselves because we feel it's unethical or someone is more qualified.

As ironic as this may seem...you're not the judge of that. The marketplace is.

When I wrote Level Up Mentality, I thought it was great. But had no clue it would be sold globally. Just put it out there. And after time, the market noticed.

The only way to get over impostor syndrome is to put it out there once you have practiced repetitively & the product is complete.

You are the product of your life.

Everything that you do comes down to connection with humans in one form or another.

Whether it's a communication with yourself or communication with the world.

Whether it's a first order, or nth order effect.

Being humble is great. Being too humble will crush your spirits over time.

Let the world know about your skills.
And maintain decorum while doing it!

Making an Enemy

June 2018 was when I started my ArmaniTalks Twitter account. Feels like it was yesterday.

A *few* months in, one of my friends discovered my account. They liked it & began following it.

A *few* more months in, a bunch of people I happened to know started following the account. One of the guys was a person who felt like we were very close. But I barely knew him.

Let's call him Chad.

Chad had this notion that we were boys & that I was going to help him in a time of need. Okay, let's see how far this goes.

Chad hops in my direct messages & is talking about a lot of his personal problems. He said that since I have empowering tweets, that I can help him solve his problems.

During that time, I would give a free 20-minute consultation call for potential clients. Chad thought he would help himself to one.

In the 20 minutes we set up, he vented away.
I gave him some practical no nonsense tips to take care of business.

But he is what I call an Ask-Hole.
They ask you for advice and do the opposite.

I wasn't pissed about this. I knew that Chad wasn't going to
be a client of mine. I just thought it would be good to help
a person out.
It's only 20 minutes of my time, all good.

However, it wasn't only 20 minutes of my time.

Chad began messaging me away after our call and was like,
'hey man, great call. When's a good to time to set up another
call with you?'

I let him know that it was only 1 free call & that was it. That's
when he pulled the *'Come on man, we are boys'* card.

Ah, I see.
A freeloader.
Seen this card pulled many times before.

I let Chad know there wasn't going to be any more future
calls and wished him the best.

This upset Chad. He felt entitled to my time and began talking
shit in my messages.

Saying stuff like, *'I don't like being ignored.'*
Acting like some crazy ex.

I found this to be amusing. Eventually, I decided to stop
responding to this clown altogether. I don't have time for that
nonsense.

A few days later, Chad blocked me and started telling my
friends that I was mean to him.

This was amusing to me. But I was irritated at the time.

Here I am, giving you a free call even though I know you wouldn't do anything with it. And now you are whining? Ungrateful piece of shit.

People irritate me at times. I have a low pain threshold for entitlement. You know, cheap people who think they deserve your time.

But what was insightful about this whole situation was how I made an enemy.

I made this enemy not by what I did.
But by what I didn't do.

I learned a big lesson that day. Younger me always thought you make an enemy when you were in the wrong. But I realized, that's not always the case.

This is why I am hesitant to believe in one side of the story before hearing the other side.
I will never fully trust human nature blindly.

I'm sure a lot of Chad and his clown ass friends thought I was some kind of cold-hearted bully.
But a few messages would have shown my innocence.

'Why not show the messages to others?'
Because there are too many people like Chad in this world. I don't have the time to explain myself to everyone.

I think character beats reputation.
Because character is how you move, and reputation is how

others think you move.

Reputation is not always in your control, but character is
always in your control.

I know if I stay true to myself, eventually, the right stuff will
work out.
*If things get hectic, I will drop receipts. Make no mistake
about that.*

However, for the most part, it's hard to get to your destination
if you get distracted by each dog that barks.

You don't need to go out and make an enemy.
Trust me, random enemies will present themselves.

Yet, our ego has us often being dragged into things that turn
out to be a waste of time.
That's how it works when entertaining an entitled person.

The world is smaller than you think. You will most definitely
run into people who you lost touch with. Social media makes
the world even smaller.

The most ironic thing about all of this was that Chad
unblocked me & apologized later. It took him over a year to
apologize. Old school Armani would have told him to kick
rocks.

Nowadays, I am growing up.
Apology accepted.

Forgiven & remembered.
'Isn't it forgive & forget?'

That's an incorrect platitude.

If I forget, then someone will waste my time twice. I remember bud. Although I won't let you know.

Enemies are presented for a reason. It seems like they pop up in harmony to each new chapter of life.

The enemy you had in high school is a different type than the one you face now. Sort of like in Dragon Ball Z, where the hero's always fight a new villain.

Every hero is a villain in someone's story.
That's the price of keeping it real.

If you chase reputation over character, you will always be putting on this persona to be liked.

Flip it.

Let people who believe the Chad's before hearing you out, leave. Be the first to show them the door.

The more we mature, the more we realize, it's not about accumulating friends. It's about reducing the circle in size.

So, reduce the circle in size.
Enemies are a part of human nature as the wind is a part of nature.

Embrace them and allow them to leave you unbothered so you can bring out your best self.

Outrage Culture

One of the best ways to get to know someone's internal world
is by looking at their social media.

Their social media is a platform that they
have **complete** power. They get to make the rules & shed their
real-life opinions.

The question is, what are they saying?

If you follow a ton of people on social media, you'll notice it's
mainly negative. They pretty much use Twitter as a diary
where they cry and act like the world is ending.

In the Universe of Twitter, the self-improvement niche is
simply a moon.

Meaning that it's tiny.

But the other planets?
Solar systems?
Galaxies?

Trolls, whiners & victims.

I have ArmaniTalks Twitter & I have a personal one where I
use to catch up with a few old friends. Every time I log into
my personal account, it seems like they are upset by
something.

'Can't believe Trump tweeted that today.'
'We live in such a racist world.'

'I am so oppressed.'

Blah blah blah.

All tweets talking about others. They routinely take the bait of
the latest sensationalist headline the mainstream media
throws out & are too unaware to even tell.

All tweets being written out & subtly reprogramming their
subconscious mind. And that polluted subconscious mind
jades their conscious thoughts.

That's why we live in the outrage culture. Negativity is
nowadays able to spread at scale.

I want to drop some reality for you...

There is the wind & the sailor.

The sailor riding his ship along a smooth sea. Out of nowhere,
the clouds get dark & the rain starts pouring in. Wind,
lightning & a whole lot of waves.

The sailor is losing control of the ship!

But now he is 100% locked in because he knows losing
control will be the end of his life.

He focuses, gets back control & maneuvers around the waves.

Soon enough, the waves die off & he gets back on track.

The wind is the external world.
The sailor is you.

The external world will never be predictable. It's always going to have an element of surprise.

Sometimes, the surprise will *favor* you.
Sometimes, it will not.

But ultimately, it's our duty to take care of business anyways.

I say all that to say this:
Focus on focusing.

Not sure if you are aware…. But the world is being designed to capture your attention.

The mainstream media designs shock headlines to get the consumer to react & reel them in like a fish.

Marketing companies point out pain points to the consumer to get them to buy.

And social media consists of a large segment of people sharing their best moments. Results?

The already scared consumer sees the great moments from someone else's life & mistakes it as the bigger picture. Causing the consumer to get jealous.

If this person continues to take the bait each time & react, then the wind is in charge.

Sad!

The real goal of this person is to be unphased by the winds & use it as an opportunity to become a better sailor. Only then will this poor individual grow.

The world lacks skilled sailors.

It's not enough to be the person whining about shit that doesn't have an impact on their life. Rather, work towards something.

Success is defined as having an idea of where you're going and making incremental progress every day.

Make the progress bud. While everyone is caught up in the noise, build your legacy.

Small wins will add up.

Soon, you'll have a big win that will have the world thinking that you were an *'overnight success.'*

That's the skilled sailor in the chaotic winds of life.

Self-Education

It was November 1st, 2008, and I sat at home staring at a textbook. It was a school day.

'So why weren't you at school?'
Because I had just gotten suspended.

'Why?'
Because I got caught skipping class with my friend, Ditra.

Not going to lie, but this one of the only times I wished I was back in school.

I sat in my kitchen trying to use the week of suspension to get caught up with all my schoolwork. I wanted to come back & begin KILLING it.

After the recent suspension, I had sealed my reputation as a failure in the IB program.

But I couldn't focus. The subjects were too damn boring!

When my parents went to work, I decided that I needed to call Ditra. I needed to find out what he was doing to kill time.

ring ring

'**Yo, whatsup bro. Listen, my dad said I can't talk to you while I'm suspended**' Ditra whispered.

"Listen, this will be quick. But what are you doing to kill time?"

'I'm reading.'

"Damn, I see that your parents took away the TV & PS2 as well, right?"

'Nah bro, I'm just reading for fun.'

"For fun?? What are you reading?"

'I am reading a book about Abraham Lincoln.'

"What the fuck? Why?"

'Because he interests me man. Why don't you give it a try?'

"Come on man. I was calling you because I didn't want to read. Anyways, thanks man."

I hung up the phone & was a little confused. Why the hell was he reading a book about Abraham Lincoln?

Ditra was definitely wasting his time!

Back to the present moment.

For my 27th birthday, my roommate had gotten me a book. It was Kobe Bryant's book regarding the Mamba Mentality. He had never gotten me a gift before.

Here I was at age 27, delighted to get a book. A decade earlier, a gift like this would have repulsed me.

'What changed?'
My desire.

You see, when I got suspended, I was reading a textbook that

I had no interest in whatsoever.

Were the subjects important? Maybe.
But I had little desire to learn them.

So, at that time, it was unfathomable to me that Ditra could
be reading a book for fun.

Made no sense!

But I didn't look into his desire. Ditra was always a big fan of
Abraham Lincoln.

You ever heard the question, 'Who is your favorite president?'

Well, he would automatically say Abraham Lincoln. But he
had no clue why.

He realized he would just default to Abraham Lincoln because
he was one of the most well-known presidents. This led Ditra
to study Lincoln so his opinion had some credibility.

A few years later, I am a firm believer that the real world is
about **unlearning** a lot of what we were taught in school.

For many years, I was seen as the dumb kid. Sucked at
standardized exams. Did awful on the SATs. Studied my ass
off to get B's and C's.

But when I left school, the game had changed. Now it was
about **me** following **my** interests.

When that happened, rather than learning with my head, I
learned with my heart. That's where self-education is different
from education.

1. Education is when you learn something because you have to.

2. Self-education is when you learn because you want to.

What's weird is that the first group often has an arrogant attitude towards knowledge.

I went to a party recently and asked a few of the guys when was the last time they read a book. They looked at me like I had 3 heads.

'Why the fuck would we read a book Armani? We aren't in school.'

There are people who genuinely think like this.
They think that just because they have a degree, that means they have learned all they need to learn.

When they are told to learn more by their managers or what not, they feel like they are doing something brutal.

But people who self-educate? Completely different.

They learn with their heart.
They follow their curiosity & sees where it takes them.

- o **One group thinks they know everything.**
- o **One group thinks they have yet to know anything.**

The thing with learning is that it is designed for a student to grow at infinite levels.

The student only stops once the desire & curiosity dims.

A famous philosopher once said:
-the learned are rattled when the world changes.
-the learners adapt when the world changes.

Use boredom as a CLUE.

If you are bored, then it's a clue that you may be self-educating yourself on the wrong thing.

When you are learning about something that truly speaks to you, the learning process is effortless. You feel pulled towards it, rather than being pushed towards it.

Analyze your body & follow the curiosities. Do that & you will learn at infinite levels.

The Accidental Life Lesson

A few years ago, I heard the quote:
"In order to get where you want to go, you need to know where you are."

Something like that.

Honest truth? Thought the quote was pure bullshit.

Why would I want to focus on the present? People who dream big are mainly focusing on the future, no?

Well, I was going to learn this lesson one day or another.

The Lost Roads

A few years back, I ended up getting settled into a new apartment in downtown Tampa. Terrific area right by the heart of the city.

After moving to this new place, I realized that it was the perfect opportunity to instill new habits.

One habit was waking up at 5 am every day to walk & do some visualization.

Well, one morning, I got up at 5 am, turned on my music & began walking.

I got so much in the zone, that I was just walking & walking, faster & faster...

Felt like I lost a track of reality.

After 30 minutes, I realized I had no clue where I was. I check my phone to turn on G Maps on how to get back, but I was on 1%.

Fuck...

It was so early in the morning that there was no one in sight. How the hell was I supposed to get back?

Well, I did what any sane person would do.

I began walking & trying to feel out the streets. I would try 1 road, then another & another.

Each road made me feel more lost.

After multiple failed attempts, something began to change.

Each new road I entered, I felt as though I got more insights.

At this point, my irritation was becoming a chip on my shoulder.

It was around 7:30ish am and more people were now entering the roads. It would have been easy to ask for directions.

But a part of me wanted to figure it out on my own. So, I chose to lock in & keep going at it. Failed road after failed road allowed me to get closer to glory.

After 2-3 hours of searching and failing, I was able to find
my way back.

At that moment, the quote from earlier flashed into my mind.

*"In order to get where you want to go, you need to know
where you are."*

And it finally clicked.

That day, I knew I wanted to get back home. But the only
problem was that I had no clue where I was in the first place.

Unfortunately, that's how many people, including myself,
have set goals.

If I know where I am, then getting to where I want to go is
like using G Maps. If I have no clue where I am, then getting
to where I want to go is blurry as heck.

Now I get it.
Challenges make winners.

But it's important to know that we will face many challenges
as we are chasing the goal. Which is why it is highly
imperative to eliminate wasted movements that can be easily
avoided.

You have the vision.
Pause.

Where are you?

Be grateful for the strengths but finish the job by being aware of the areas of improvement.

After you do so, a part of you will feel fuller & more
ambitious to keep the journey going.

You won't feel lost, entering street to street. But rather, a path
is set up. And now you are simply walking forward.

Why Listening Is More Powerful Than Speaking

Listening is more important than speaking. My mindset was not always like this.

I used to be a very shy kid when I was younger. And my shyness worsened when I had the speaking over listening mentality.

Thought the success of a social interaction was determined by who could say the coolest things.

- o This led to years & years of overthinking.
- o The overthinking led to under talking.
- o The under talking led to a *fly on the wall* treatment.

'So let me get this straight. You're telling me a shy kid should NOT focus on speaking?'
Correct.

If they focus on speaking first, then they will overthink.

When things began to change

After years & years of failed social interactions, I realized that it was time to do some soul searching.

What am I missing?
How come I can't figure this out?

I decided that I was going to do something much different. I was going to **observe**.

At this point, I had a *few* friends who were very charismatic. They were well known, well liked & could make friends seamlessly.

Was it their looks?
Their clothes?
Their cologne?

No....

All these charismatic people had one common characteristic.

I noticed they didn't really talk that much.

They mainly listened, showed interest & would contribute strategically. Their interest paired with their listening skills allowed them to contribute points that made you think.

Points that flowed perfectly with the conversation. Points that made their counterpart feel **heard**.

At that point, everything clicked!!

Charisma wasn't about getting other people to like you. Charisma was about getting other people to like themselves.

How Listening Makes you a Better Speaker

I spent the next *few* months altering my strategy. At this stage, it was about listening OVER speaking.

'Any improvements?'

Yes! Now it was much easier to flow in the social world.

I took the spotlight off me and put the spotlight on the other person. This killed 2 birds with 1 stone.

I was no longer feeling so much pressure and the other person felt like a star!

Once my mind was at ease, it became much easier to speak. Plus, the words were much more valuable because I wasn't yapping away the whole conversation.

The fact that I showed interest in the other person made them more receptive to show interest in me. The social world finally began to make more sense.

Changing your Mindset

The listening over speaking mindset will have you viewing life in a vastly different way. You will no longer be in a rush to talk.

Rushing to talk comes with built in anxiety.
It creates the *'will I live up to expectations??'* mentality.

A mentality which is very far from social intelligence.

Talking is a subconscious act.
It can be done on autopilot.
Listening is a conscious act.
It cannot be done on autopilot.

Hearing is physical and listening is mental.

With hearing, the senses are engaged, sure.

But the mind can be in lala land.
That's not listening bud.

For the listening perception to be complete, the mind needs to be connected to the senses of hearing and information needs to be digested.

Listening is a true focus sharpener. It's difficult.
That's why so few opt to do it. And their social intelligence suffers.

Anything we place value on is anything that we place attention on.

Younger me placed more value on speaking than listening.
Which caused listening to be a tension full process.

Older me learned that by valuing listening over speaking, the speaking takes care of itself.
Now listening became a tension free process.

Practice makes perfect, sure. But in order to change your mindset regarding listening, you need to understand the VALUE of the act.

Not because I told you to understand the value.
Instead, because the words I am writing right now, lead to a PERSONAL revelation from your end.

Why Being Selfish is a Good Thing

A few years ago, I was stuck between 2 roads.

I didn't know which path to choose:
Selfish or Selfless?

My entire life, I was told by society that being selfless was the way to go. Be selfless & good things will happen to you Armani!

Just give back & people will do the same.
'So did you do it?'
Yes.

I spent years as the 'nice guy.'

You know, the guy who is a pushover, giggles at everything & is a people pleaser?

Well, that was me.

I genuinely thought being nice was going to get me ahead in life. I was bound to get ahead soon, right?

Wrong.

To my shock, the exact opposite began to happen.

I wasn't respected by my fellow peers. I wasn't getting ahead. Most importantly, I was not feeling happy.

Society lied to me by saying I needed to be selfless. Well, let me rephrase that.

Society *misguided* me by telling me that I needed to be selfless.

Being selfless was needed. But first, I needed to be selfish.

Altered Path

When I was a selfless from the get-go, I became a nice guy. Why?

Because I had nothing to offer.

I hadn't invested enough energy in building myself up. How could I possibly have provided value to others when I couldn't even provide value to myself? My service was subpar at best.

That's when I learned strategic selfishness.

1. Look out for your own needs first.

2. Invest in yourself.

3. Get comfortable saying no so you can work on your dreams.

In the selfish stage, I was consuming & leveling up to an insane level. The goal was to become my grandest self. This is the art of becoming VALUABLE.

Selfish -> Selfless

When I spent a long period being selfish, I got the goal of having created value for myself.

Put some respect on my name!

NOW it was time to be selfless.

When a person takes time to build value for themselves, giving value is much easier. It does not require much conscious thought. A lot of times, value is provided subconsciously.

Valuable people provide value by accident.

This person of value becomes different. Everything they touch turns into gold. They breathe life into the dead. The inspire people around them.

What sounds better to you, the needy nice guy or the beacon of hope?

No brainer.

Embrace your Selfish Stage

If you are skipping the selfish stage to be selfless, you are not doing anyone any good.

The world doesn't need any more subpar talent. They need people who excel in their craft.

Be selfish.
Learn, create, build.

Then, be selfless.
Teach, help, inspire.

That's how the game was meant to be played.

What is a Genius?

I think it was Kanye West who was the first person I heard use the term 'creative genius.'
I thought he was being awkward when he used that phrase.

Creative genius?? Is that even a thing?
How can you be a genius for being creative?
You can't measure that creativity....

Silly rabbit.

Growing up, I thought a genius was someone who excelled in academics. Someone who had a high IQ, did killer in the SAT's & got straight A's.

'Are you saying you were wrong?'
Nope. I was partially correct.

After I had graduated from school & went off to the real world, I was an electrical engineer. A logical guy that was supposed to fix.

Well, that was at least what I thought.

Engineering as a Creative Act?

The first day I had gotten into work, my manager was teaching me the ropes about designing new systems, code & circuity.

There was rarely any fixing. You mean I was supposed to innovate?

It was my first job that taught me that creativity was much more important than I gave it credit for.

Creativity was not some bland act.
It was the lifeblood of innovation.

The Definition of Genius

A genius is defined as:
"Someone with exceptional intellectual or creative power or other natural ability."

You see that?
Intellectual OR creative power.

Kanye West was not crazy.
He was just spitting facts.
'What if I don't like Kanye's music. How do I know he is a genius?'
Doesn't matter whether you like him or not.
HE thinks he's a genius.

A creative genius is much more different than an intellectual genius.

- o   *An intellectual genius can be measured with tests.*
- o   *A creative genius is measured by their innovation.*

When I learned about the creative genius terminology, my entire world had shaken up.

Can YOU be a Genius too?

Of course, you can be a genius. But the question is, do you think that you can be?

Because I used to rule myself out. Thought genius was out of my realm.

Nowadays, I realized that I just need my imagination & the rest is history.

'Do you consider yourself a genius?'
Absolutely. I need to, otherwise I won't be able to produce at a high level. And you should consider yourself a genius too. Because here's the thing, once you KNOW that you are a genius, you unlock a different side to you.

You start producing quality & quantity.
You start innovating.
You start changing lives.
You shake up the ENTIRE world.

That's how you make reality bend to your will.
It all begins with the narrative that you set for yourself. If you don't think you are a genius, then you aren't. If you think you are a genius, then you will be.

Don't let society dictate your label.
Architect it yourself.
Your legacy awaits.

Knowing your Audience

Culture plays a big role in communication.

Whether you are giving a speech.
Writing an email.
Or trying to spread a social message.

Culture plays a huge role. Need to know the audience. Let me tell you a story.

I was asked to be a keynote speaker for a graduation a few years ago. The host told me to just 'share my story.'

Thought that was a vague direction. But oh well, let's see where I could take it. Decided to call the speech **5 lessons**.

Overall, it was a story about the lessons I learned from moving to a new country, learning English, and finding a way to get adjusted.

Delivered the 10-minute speech & awaited the response.

It was well received.

This surprised me.

'Why?'
Because a few weeks ago, the same speech was not well received. After my prior talk, the audience was indifferent.

The speech hadn't changed.
'So, what did?'
The interpretation.

The first audience consisted of people who never had a significant move in their life. They lived in the same country for a long time.

But the second audience had a bunch of people who left their home country to start over in the US.

The second crowd was able to **resonate** with my story.

"Resonate" is a BIG word in the public speaking world.

Resonating is when the audience felt in **tune** with you.

You can do that by sharing a story that relates to them.

Or tying your story into an analogy which relates to them.

Factor in culture.

Where are they from?
Age group?
What are their interests?
Anything about their past you should know?

The more you know the audience, the more the speech crafts itself.

The mainstream media used to enforce a certain culture. But with the rise of the internet, culture has become fragmented. It's more about micro communities now.

Having just an idea of who will be in your audience can make a night or day sort of difference for your speech.

Understand life from their eyes so they can

understand life from your yours.

How to Build Influence

Influence is defined as the capacity to have an effect on the behavior of someone else.

Pretty powerful when you think about it.

Everyone wants to build influence. But only a few put in the work.

You often see markets getting saturated. No matter what industry you are in. The participants look around and think there is a lot of competition.

But look closer. How many of those people are actually serious?

When you look closer, you will often see most of the people have half foot in and half foot out. They are lollygagging & moving in circles.

Are they elevating? Nah, not all of them.
Only a few are.

That's why Pareto Principle is the principle of human nature. It's always just a few who rise to the top.

There are hundreds of soda companies around the world.
But there is only one Coca Cola.

There are tons of players in the NBA.
But only a few superstars.

There are tons of online retail companies.
But only one Amazon.

The reason Pareto principle holds true time and time again is because human nature always kicks in.

-Laziness is a subconscious act.
-And hard work is a conscious one.

Humans are wired to take the path of least resistance.

When I was young, I wondered why the richest people on Earth just didn't spread out their money to everyone in the world. In that case, everyone would win! Right?

Nah, wrong.

The same people will end up getting their money back. It's because money is simply a byproduct of their knowledge, street smarts & habits.

They are wired this way.

Not saying the people who are less fortunate don't deserve the money. What I'm saying is that the solution isn't always as easy as it seems.

Which brings me to the title:
How does one build influence?

By showing up every day.

There should be a path that you are walking. And each day you should be taking a minimum of a step. That's it.

o   One day, you'll take 30 steps.

o   Another day, you'll take 1300 steps.

o   And one day, you'll take 1 step.

All the steps are adding up in the right direction.

As you take these steps, others are going to get curious & be like:

'Where is this fellow walking? And why are they walking with such conviction? They may be onto something! I'll follow them.'

That bystander will follow you. It just begins with 1 follower.

Humans follow humans who are followed by other humans.

That's another life law.

When I got my first follower on Twitter, I was happy. But he was my best friend. He was supposed to follow me. All good. A follower is a follower.

It's just been a matter of staying consistent every day. Now I have 25,000+ followers.

This isn't to brag.

Instead, to show you that it is all about having a vision & taking incremental steps towards that vision.

Influence is simply a byproduct of you following a genuine passion.

They look at you & wonder how you make it look so easy. But

little do they know... you are just having fun.

If I didn't have a single follower, subscriber or reader, I'd still do what I do. It's because I enjoy it.

I've never shitted on people who have a 40 hour a week job. Because if you enjoy something, you enjoy it.

If influence is what you're chasing, then you are playing the wrong game.

Chase your best self.

Everything else is secondary. That's how influence begins chasing you.

50 Cent vs. Kanye West

In 2000s, 50 Cent declared a competition against Kanye West. He said, if Kanye sells more records than him, then he would retire.

This was big news.

Around that time, 50 Cent was on top of the hip hop world. The man was a hit making machine. Kanye? He was on the come up.

In the competition, it was clear that Kanye West was the underdog. He was gifted in his own right.

However, there were still levels.

It came to many people's shock that once the numbers came in; it wasn't what the general public expected.

50 Cent didn't blow Kanye West out.

Instead, Kanye was the one with leading numbers in the first week.

It's strange how that moment is forgotten in hip hop history.

To take it a level further, many have no clue that 50 Cent was even a rapper.

For people born in the late 90s, early 20s, 50 Cent is a businessman. They forget he used to be as big if not bigger than Drake during 2003.

50 Cent & Kanye both started off as rappers alone. But they expanded.

-50 Cent went on to film with his hit show, Power.
-Kanye went on to design with his hit shoes, Yeezy's.

From the outside, these 2 both seem like creative geniuses. When looking closer, their creative genius stems from different sources.

50 Cent is from the material realm.
Kanye is from the divine realm.

What's the difference between material & divine realm?

Material realm is more externally focused.
Divine realm is more internally focused.

During 50 Cent's career, he's always been involved in some kind of beef. From Ja Rule, Fat Joe, Jadakiss, French Montana, Oprah etc.

To take it even a level further, he seems to even beef with his loved ones. G-Unit is no more, he doesn't have a strong relationship with his first born, his baby mother etc.

This isn't to degrade him. More so explain why he is externally focused.

The first thing that I remember hearing about him was that he got shot 9 times. A guy who gets shot 9 times AND survives has a different mindset than the average person.

The average person is already focused on the material world.

We are focused on our bodies. When we think about our

bodies, we associate that with safety. When we are safety focused, we strengthen the ego.

50 Cent has a strong ego which has led to a lot of his success in the business world.

You remember what it's like when you feel like your back is against the wall?

Picture yourself studying the night before an important exam. That's when you supercharge learning skills that were initially dormant.

A person with a strong ego has the capability to unlock extreme creative powers.

They always feel like someone is coming to take everything away from them.

In my opinion, this has been the case for 50 Cent.

Advantage: Strong creativity.
Disadvantage: A lot of damaged relationships along the way.

For Kanye West, his attention seems to be more internal.

I call the internal the divine creativity just for word choice that I normally associate with. You can just call it internal creativity. Don't get too caught up in the words.

This is when the focus is on the internal world.
You aren't necessarily so focused on what others are doing in your creation process. Instead, you are extremely focused on you.

This is one of the reasons why Kanye has produced a lot of

music that seemed to be pushing the hip hop culture in new directions.

One famous quote is, 'We miss the Old Kanye.'

The Old Kanye represented traditional hip hop.

New Kanye has a different style to him.

One of my friends who went to his concert said it felt like some Shakespeare show. Something WAY out there in terms of hip hop.

Advantage: Strong creativity.
Disadvantage: Potential to go crazy.

The thoughts are not anchored (yet). Therefore, it's easier to go from thought to thought like a tornado. Without an anchor, a hyper inflated ego may form.

'What is this anchor that you speak of?'
A purpose to give your thoughts direction. Like a north star. A cause bigger than you.

In Kanye's case, it was religion.

Recently, he has been going back to his religious roots. I believe that serves as a staple for his thoughts.

50 Cent and Kanye West are both gifted, no denying that. But there never is all good without any sacrifice. Good & bad come together champ.

Which type of creativity do you resonate with?

For my brand, I resonate more with internal creativity.

I don't really care what others are doing too much. I respect them. But don't use them as a barometer to make my moves.

What about you?

Having a rough understanding starts allowing you to create your own creativity blueprint.

Dealing with Negative Feedback

In 2012, there was a new hookah place that had opened up around my college.

The owner of this hookah spot was a Pakistani man who was 5 years older. I was 20 years old at the time.

He just moved to Tampa from Texas and didn't know anyone. I discovered the place when I went looking for coals on a very late night.

When I went, I was surprised to see the place was EMPTY. I talked to the Pakistani guy, Sean.

He said he didn't know anyone in the town & business had been slow. I was in a fraternity around the time and was the events coordinator.

A part of me wanted to introduce a bunch of people to this awesome hookah spot.

I told Sean to be ready on Friday, I was going to bring a lot of people.

Friday ended up being packed.

The hookah bar was so nice that others started telling their friends about it. They also wanted to be the first to break the news.

As a few weeks went by, Sean's hookah bar was unrecognizable. Sometimes, there were so many people that there was a line to wait on.

Good problem to have.

Sean came to me & expressed gratitude.

He's like, *'I gotta thank you Armani for getting me started. In order to express gratitude, I am going to name a hookah flavor after you.'*

I thought he was joking.
But no! He was serious.

That night, after a bunch of experimenting, **Armani XXX was born.**

That hookah meant a lot to my college self.

During that time, I didn't have much of an identity. So having a hookah named after me gave me a lot of clout.

Eventually, a bunch of people were smoking it. It felt good hearing 'Let me get that Armani.'

Well, one person didn't like it too much.

His name was Farook.

Truth be told, Farook didn't even smoke hookah.

'Then why did he hate it?'
Because he hated me.

I used to hook up with Farook's sister back then & he didn't like it. I didn't owe this guy anything. Barely ever talked to him.

But rather than talk face to face, he'd gossip about me. He was my number 1 hater in college.

One day, as a bunch of us are chilling in the hookah bar, Farook blurts out:

'Armani, your hookah flavor sucks!!'

I was livid.

Especially seeing that he didn't take a puff since we had been at the bar. He just wanted to run his mouth for the sake of running it.

My younger self wanted to whoop his ass. But I didn't want to fight in Sean's bar like that.

So, I gave Farook a nickname.
I called him the 'Little Man.'

Farook was a little man & just calling him that multiple times eventually *made it stick.*

Eventually, everyone would call him the 'Little Man' in a joking way. But Farook didn't find it funny.

It branded him.

No girls want to hook up with the 'Little Man.'
No one takes the opinion of a 'Little Man' seriously.

Not only physically little. But the brand implied his personality was *small.*

I felt like I had gotten my revenge & won.

As time went on & I started to mature, I realized there was a lot to learn. Armani XXX was a public hookah. Others were allowed to have opinions regarding it.

To take it a level further, I was the External Vice President for my fraternity at the time (the guy who threw events). So, people were allowed to have opinions regarding me.

Hurting Farook's rep like that felt very good at the time. I think he learned his lesson.

In 2020, I saw Farook at a wedding & we had a good laugh about the whole thing.

He is much calmer now and we are both on good terms.

Dealing with criticism is never easy. How should a person deal with it?

My suggestion is to first evaluate if it's criticism or if it's straight hate.

I would constitute Farook as a hater. For individuals like that, ignoring is the best.

Sometimes, you need to check someone when they are being too disrespectful. Which is why I don't regret what I did.

There is a fine line of checking someone though.

When you are in building mode, checking everyone who talks shit becomes a very draining experience. It's hard to be a creator AND a checker.

More often than not, you can wear one hat at a time. Unless you combine the 2 hats.

'Meaning?'
Well, the whole 'Little Man' thing was a combination of a creator and a check.

I **created** a nick name for him. And that ended up getting him to fall back. **Checked**.

That's playing with fire though. Because sometimes humans don't fall back.

A person whose ego has been deeply wounded may pull a kamikaze. They'll go down (because they have nothing else to lose) just for the pleasure of taking you down.

If you consider yourself a funny person, then make light of haters. Turn them into a joke & they will get agitated that they aren't getting under your skin. Being able to laugh at yourself is a superpower.

However, it's important to be aware of legitimate criticism.

Critics are not intentionally being mean people.
They just want you, the product or service to be better.

One of the people I was cool with thought Armani XXX was too sweet.

That's feedback.
A negative feedback.
But feedback, nevertheless.

Calling this individual a hater would have shown poor social intelligence on my end.

Evaluate the opinion and see if you want to apply it.

Notice the latter part. 'SEE if you want to apply it.'

Just because you get a negative feedback doesn't mean you automatically do what they say.

That's why self-awareness is key in picking up when someone is right or when someone is wrong.

Even more awareness is needed is to pick up when you're wrong.

It's a constant fine-tuning process.

I heard this quote that made me realize who to put more importance on:

-Would you rather be at war with yourself & at peace with the world?

Or

-Would you rather be at peace with yourself & at war with the world?

The person in the mirror will have to ponder on this one.

How to Gain Respect

'What's more powerful, respect or attention?'
Respect is more powerful.

Yet, it takes time to gain.

There's a certain baseline amount of respect that respectable people give to others.

That's the standard amount.

When you pile more respect on top of that standard, it leads to a brand.

A brand can be a surplus of respect or disrespect.
Whatever the case is, it's not on the standard state.

If it was on the standard state, then the brand doesn't stick out. It would just be white noise for the subconscious mind.

Respect is powerful & it is simplicity that gets it.

It happens when the brand is not being a 'try hard.'

A 'try hard' is someone who does too much. They don't seem authentic because it seems like they are just trying to shock others. I call them the purposeful polarizers.

I had to get a Tik Tok account when it was first blowing up, because 2 of my clients wanted to build a brand there. I downloaded the app to stay on top of their progress. To see how well they were speaking in front of the camera.

As I looked through the content on Tik Tok, I saw a lot of attention seeking.

People hitting others on the face with purses.
Making weird jokes. And a whole bunch of random shocking challenges.

A lot of entertainment is based off attention first. I'm not hating on that.

A brand is being built all the time.
Online and/or offline.

Example:
Let's say you go to a networking event with a wrinkly shirt on.

This will negatively impact your brand.

'But I wasn't trying to rep anything at all!'

That's not an option bud. If you have a body, then others will form perceptions of you.

Gaining respect happens by:
-Being consistent
-Being an empowering energy

Being Consistent

It's crazy how many people hated Kobe Bryant around 2004-5ish. It was NOT cool to like him at all.

But what could you say about his game?
He was consistently at the top.

By the time he announced his retirement, even the rival Celtics fans were giving him a standing ovation for a stellar career.

Being consistent means being in it for the long run.

Others are not going to respect you the entire time. Heck, they may blatantly hate you for certain periods!

The great one's show up regardless.

That's when the public builds an emotional bond with the great one, causing the perception to warp.

Consistency gives respect as long as the person keeps adding value to their field.

Being an Empowering Energy

I used to be a part of a business networking group in Tampa.

I was new to the group, so was still building my brand with the other members.

Well, one of the veteran members found my YouTube channel & she enjoyed the videos. She would routinely tell others in the business networking group how great the videos were and to subscribe to my channel.

#1, I gained respect for her because her endorsement gave me more credibility.

#2, others respected her because they could see that she wanted others to win.

#3, she gained respect for herself because she conditioned abundance mindset into her subconscious mind.

The people who value attention too much are the ones who will willingly act like a clown.

By the way, it's smart to not seek respect too much. Then becoming a tyrant is inevitable.

Some people want respect so much to a point where any criticism gets them heated. And that person loses more respect after each tirade.

High value will come as long as a person keeps doing what they said they were going to do.

The secret truth is, often, we don't feel confident because we don't really respect ourselves.

'Why is that?'
Because we begin tasks, but don't finish it.

Finishing 1 task is better than beginning 10 and leaving them unfinished.

When you finish a task, you know that you are a doer.

You don't always have to announce when you are going to do something. But if you feel like you have been slacking, then maybe you should make it public.

Let's say Paul tried to pick up a diet undercover and failed 2 weeks in. Then Paul should think about telling 15 people that he is going on a diet.

If Paul has the drive, he will be consistent & hit his targets.

His pride is involved.

Once he builds respect with himself, he will build respect with others.

As Paul starts to gradually gain more and more respect for himself, that's when an addiction begins to form. The good kind of addiction.

He slowly stops caring whether he wins others over or not.

Wow. A feedback loop has been activated. Paul becomes more consistent.

As Paul feels better about himself, he starts spreading empowering energy like my friend did for me in the networking group.

That's how respect becomes an emergent property rather than the goal in itself.

Reading a Book a Week

The average CEO reads 52 books a year. Which equates to a book a week. This sounds like a mythical number, until you realize it's not.

Reading a book a week is perfectly doable.

You don't need speed reading gifts for it either.
You just need determination and a strategy.

'Is the strategy difficult?'
Not at all.

1. Divide the book into 5 parts.
2. Aim to finish it by the weekdays.
3. If you can't finish it by the weekdays, then use your weekends to finish.

Boom, you're done.

This seems like an easy strategy, but only a few can manage.

From my estimate, it requires 45 minutes to 1.5 hour reading a day depending on the size of the book.
(numbers can vary tremendously based on focus levels & reading pace).

'Have you done it?'
Yep, plenty of times. I still do this tactic.

-Great writers are great readers.

-Great speakers are great watchers.

Top athletes watch their game back after they are done playing.

The basketball player Chris Paul watches as much basketball as he can. From college all the way to the professionals.

Reading a book a week is a fun challenge because it develops linguistics intelligence.
Linguistics intelligence is the gift with words.
It's broken down to:
- **Consumption** : Reading, Listening.
- **Production** : Writing, Speaking.

The easy target of splitting a book into 5 gives the mind a clear objective. If you have the determination, this is perfectly doable.

Don't rush. Read with a gentle pace that allows you to understand.

Do You Understand What You're Learning?

"Assimilate" is defined as the process of taking something fully in.

To assimilate information means to truly learn something.

There is a group who consumes a lot of information. But their behaviors don't match.
Why is that?

It can be due to a lack of experiences and/or dwelling.

Experiences are self-explanatory. You need to eventually get to a point when you are taking the effort to apply the information.

Dwelling is something that can be a bit more confusing. *So, let's make sure we are on the same page.*

Dwelling is a word with a negative connotation to it.
That's because we are using our personal memory in correlation to this word. When we think of dwelling, we think of replaying a mistake from our past.

On the other hand, a lot of super learners view dwelling as drying the cement.
-The act of dwelling isn't bad.
-What you are dwelling on will determine if you have a good or bad experience.

I used to know this kid in my engineering class
who **never** took notes. Yet, he would score super high grades
on each exam.

I on the other hand had a whole bunch of notes.
But nothing but Cs to show for it. What gives?

Well, this guy told me that notes would distract him from his
mind & the professor. Why introduce a barrier?

His strategy was completely different. He would read the
lecture the night before. Then, during the lecture on class day,
he would just make a few mental notes when his body FELT
something that the teacher said.

The points that his body felt were the points he deemed worth
dwelling over. And that, he did.

When I asked him what he meant by dwelling, he made it
sound so simple:
*'I pretty much do as little as I possibly can with the
information.'*
He was trying to imply that dwelling in his world is different
than introspecting.

Introspecting requires work.
Like you are going through Google scouring for the right
answer for something.

Dwelling is more passive.
You found a great movie. Now you're just sitting back and
watching. Doing too much will distract you from the movie.

For dwelling, he would just say that he wants his mind to go over this point a *few* times and reflect on that point.

The more he would reflect on that point, the more he would turn the wet cement of the information into concrete. Assimilating the information.

It's like cooking.

When you just toss unseasoned chicken into the oven, it tastes like crap.
If you marinate the chicken for 10 seconds & throw it in the oven, it still tastes a bit weird.

But if you marinate the chicken & let it rest for a few hours, then throw it in the oven, it ends up tasting great. That's because you gave the chicken time to absorb the flavor. This is how it works with information too!

The thing with our mind is that it naturally dwells, normally inclined towards negative thoughts. Reprograming the mind to dwell on something productive requires **constant** repetition.

I had all the notes in the world during school...
But I never assimilated it.

I thought writing a bunch of junk on a piece of paper meant that I would getting smarter.
While I was just collecting junk.

This friend of mine learned like this:

1. Get a holistic idea of the subject (reading the class lecture

the night before).

2. Zone in on the crucial points (allowing his feelings to
signal to him which points stuck out in context to his prior
day reading).

3. Assimilate the idea through a blend of experience &
dwelling.

Dwelling should feel effortless.
Go for relaxation.

The more relaxed you are, the more the subconscious mind
starts to absorb the information.

The best tip is to start off the movement cycle. Keep getting
the experience. Dwelling at this point is not making sense.

But once you get the momentum rolling, you'll notice
dwelling on the information naturally happens.

Keep repeating the information.

Dwelling on your free time makes it easier to assimilate the
information. This compounds the knowledge for the future
which amplifies judgement.

At this point, memorizing is no longer viewed as learning.
Instead, memorizing is just one chapter of the whole learning
book.

How Breakups Make You Stronger

The beauty about breakups is that it forces you to make a significant life choice. The life choice comes down to: *Leveling up or down.*

This may seem like an oversimplification, but not really.

If you analyze your past breakups or are going through one now, then look closer.

The traditional route is to level down... at first. (I will explain the 'at first' portion shortly).

At this stage, you are sad, lazy, go on a drinking spree and all of that.

To be honest, this is normal & often necessary. Not the 3 traits that I listed above, but some form of leveling down is fine because it allows you to process what happened.

Your emotions are overwhelming your body & your mind is trying to adjust with the internal energy.

This is why you're finding it hard to sleep, eat & get excited about stuff.

After you have had time to process the energy, you **must** ask yourself what the next step is?

Some will decide to level down even more! They do anything

they can to hide the pain.

But a rare group of people decide that now is the time to level up.

They will go to the gym, pick up a hobby & create something. They aren't burying the pain, rather, they are leveraging it to produce.

When you can **use** that internal energy, you have your fuel for the level up journey.

I remember Eminem once mentioned that he was creating some of his best works when he was going through rock bottom. It's because he was feeling a lot of emotions that were bringing out a different side to him.

People have a logical side & an emotional side. The logical side allows us to operate well within the realms of reality. But the emotional side allows us to shatter that reality. It makes us a lot more unpredictable, chaotic & unstructured.

'Whoa bro, that sounds like a bad thing!'
Well, it can be.

That's if you let your emotions destruct you.

But if you decide to produce with the emotions, then the 'unpredictable, chaotic & unstructured' traits become your ***creative fuel***.

Art = *Structured Chaos.*

It all begins with being emotionally intelligent. The art of finding healthy ways for the mind & heart to work **together**.

-If you lead with your brain too much, you become overly logical & neglect your intuition.

-If you lead with your heart too much, you become overly whimsical & neglect your rationale.

Life is a game of finding a balance.

Whether it's a breakup, getting over a car accident, moving on from getting fired, understand that all emotions can still help.

It all comes down to choosing the perception for that energy.

Your body's internal energy can be your fuel or anchor. The choice is yours.

Conversation Mistake

There's a conversation sin which typically goes unnoticed. It went unnoticed by me for a long time until I experienced it multiple times in one week.

'What was that mistake?'
Irrelevant questions.

On that particular week, I was having a conversation with my friend regarding public speaking.

He genuinely seemed curious, so I decided to help him with a lot of common public speaking concerns.

As we were talking, I noticed his eyes began darting out of nowhere.

(Whenever people go from strong eye contact to weak eye contact, it means they stopped paying attention.)

I continued explaining anyways on practical methods to overcome speech anxiety. By the time I was done, he responds with:

'Hey bro, been to any good restaurants lately?'

Huh??? What do restaurants have to do with public speaking?

Needless to say, I wasn't giving him any more public speaking tips after that. This wasn't about public speaking.

This is about executing the #1 responsibility in a

conversation.

'What is that?'
Paying attention.

When you pay attention, the questions seem to present themselves. You don't have to think of new questions to ask, but rather follow up further with something that was already mentioned.

In a conversation, there are 'hooks.'

Hooks are portions in a conversation that you can expand further into with questions. In many cases, people purposely leave hooks hoping for you to ask about it.

Occasionally, the conversation does dry out, which requires you to think of a brand-new question. But when someone is speaking & going out of their way to help YOU, then it's your duty to ask RELEVANT questions.

'How do you define relevancy?'
I define relevancy as the context of the question in relation with the context of the conversation.

My friend's question about restaurants wasn't a stupid question. But in the context of a conversation that dealt with public speaking?

Stupid question!

It showed that he was not paying attention & he plummeted his likability in the process.

The #1 reason a person has trouble paying attention is

because they are not curious about others. The curious mindset blazes through social anxiety, narcissism, and irrelevant questions.

There are good people who don't know any better. They try to pay attention. Too much work.

Just assume the person has information that will change your life forever. Each person has an insight that they will drop any second that will shift your world view. This leads to a curious mindset.

'Will they actually drop that insight?'
Yes.

I may be telling the truth.
I may be lying.

But I know that the mysterious insight held in the other person will lead to amplified curiosity...

The Most Polarizing Phrase on Twitter

June 2019 marked my 1-year anniversary on Twitter. It was nothing short of an adventure.

During that 1 year, I was able to make connections with people from all over the world, built a customized website & shared tons of content on soft skills. But want to know something?

Twitter has a dark side.

It is one of the many platforms that can bring out the crazies.

You probably have seen it yourself. The more viral a tweet gets, the more love AND hate it gets.

Polarization 101.

Heck, one of the accounts I follow had such a polarizing tweet that he ended up getting death threats for a week.

So needless to say, there are tons of polarizing words, thoughts & phrases on the platform.

From my experience, I noticed one phrase that was VERY polarizing.

'And what was that?'
Emotional Intelligence.

'Wait really? That word is polarizing??'

Yep, *very*.

One group loves the tweets regarding emotional intelligence because they feel like it resonates with them.

The other group hates the tweets regarding emotional intelligence & thinks it's a fake terminology designed to control people. Therefore, it's a very black or white topic.

Why the polarization?

Shouldn't everyone want to be emotionally intelligent? Using your mind & emotions to work in harmony to make rational decisions seems like a no brainer.

The common misunderstanding about emotional intelligence is that it's when you make *emotional* decisions.

Another reason for the polarization is because EQ cannot be measured, while IQ can.

So, the detractors say that EQ is nonsense & IQ is the main thing to focus on.

I'm going to challenge that thought pattern for a second. IQ is great for measuring critical thinking capabilities.

But believing that the WHOLE umbrella of intelligence is solely determined by critical thinking abilities can lead to a fixed mindset.

True intelligence is an umbrella consisting of:
  o   *Critical thinking*
  o   *Creative thinking*
  o   *Empathy*

o   *Social skills*

o   *Curiosity*

o   *Mental Toughness*

Therefore, IQ represents critical thinking.
EQ represents empathy.

'What makes empathy so crucial?'
Empathy is a sign of intellect in terms of dealing with others & yourself.

When it comes to others, the empathetic person will build stronger social bonds. When it comes to yourself, you will be able to forgive past mistakes & recondition your perception towards failures.
I do agree, EQ cannot be measured with an exam. It can be measured with your own awareness.

It's a game of leveraging self-awareness, honesty & self-correction to analyze how well you make rational decisions for your lifestyle when faced with a flurry of emotions.

How well you can regulate destructive emotions into productive fuel?

Ruling off an entire subject because it cannot be measured with an exam is a silly notion. That is also one of the main reasons that people lose touch with their intuition. They want to quantify everything with a manmade test.

Doesn't work like that in all facets of life. The world isn't so black & white, rather it is gray.

Adjust and adapt.

At the end of the day, IQ & EQ both have a place in this world.

Critical thinking is vital & will allow a person to not act like an impulsive clown. But it's important to understand that decisions which happen in a microsecond are often based on emotions, not solely logic.

How to Deal with Snakes

We like complexity because simplicity scares us. Our
entire lives, we were taught to be complex.

When we were in school, we were learning 6-7 subjects, not
one. We mainly multitasked. We played with 1 toy, before we
went searching for the next. Our fear of missing out, led us to
stay busy.

I'm here to tell you that in the real world, complexity can lead
a person to deal with an abundant of snakes!

A snake is a character in the social world known for
backstabbing. They smile to your face & talk shit behind your
back.

'Are snakes & haters the same?'
Nope.

Haters make their presence known.
Snakes try to cover their tracks.

The fact that you don't know who they are makes the day of
reckoning sting *a lot* more.

When you find out that you've been back stabbed by
someone who you had love for, it hurts. There is a sense of
betrayal, disappointment, confusion and **anger**.

The level of anger causes the victim to make their next move
very complex, rather than simple. That level of complexity is
known as *revenge*.

Revenge is the untamed ego's next plan of action for the victim.

Since this snake back stabbed them, they feel like the most effective move is to hurt them in *some* way. So, emotions and mind are used to devise a plan for revenge.

Results?
Further hurt on the victim's end.

At this point, the person who has gotten backstabbed has strayed so far from their path, that they forgot what their central mission was. All the energy could have been used on their goals, dreams or desires.

But no.
They gave it to the snake.

Want to know the saddest part? The snake feels **more** important. Often, the snake is happy that their actions caused someone else to act out of character and seek revenge.

The snake finds the efforts amusing. Humans work in weird ways.

'Damn Armani! I don't want to bring joy to the person who made me suffer. So, what should I do?'
Keep it **simple**. Quietly burn the bridge & move on.

'Wait what?? No revenge?'
Nope.
'No name calling?'
Nah.
'No gossiping?'
No!

Rather, invest all that energy back to further yourself. Snakes are abundant in the real world, my friend.

The truth is that the older you get, the less you trust. Not the other way around.

Use betrayal as a learning moment & an opportunity to toughen up. Snake bites sting, I know. But it happens to everyone who steps foot in the social arena.

Just know how to deal with them rationally, rather than impulsively.
Ignoring them requires 0 time & effort from your end. And now you have made them feel unimportant like the low-level creature that they are.

It's a win-win.

Ignoring someone who did you dirty is one of the toughest things to do. But the tougher it is, the more character it builds.

Take the road less taken.

In a few days, weeks, months, once the feeling of hurt has subsided, the feeling of joy will take its spot.

Feeling proud of yourself is the ultimate way to boost your self-confidence. So do the difficult now & reap the rewards later!

You will not be disappointed.

When Competition Goes Wrong

Let me ask you something...

Have you ever had that moment where you stacked up a major win in life... And when you were trying to tell your friend, you got a reaction that you didn't expect.

They *seem* happy for you. But when you look closer, they are thinking about something else.

What is it they are thinking about? you wonder.

As the thinking stops, rather than asking you for more details about your win, they do the exact opposite. They somehow manage to make the conversation about themself!

They talk about one of their recent wins as well. Then they begin telling you a story about it.

You are a little upset that you guys didn't discuss your win longer, but you brush it off as 'competitive spirit' from their end.

I hate people like that.
Annoying as hell.

I used to deal with a person like that when I was first starting a Shopify business a few years ago.

My friend Mikey told me about Shopify & gave me some

insights into how the business model works. Then he threw a few videos my way to help me build a stronger understanding of the business.

For the next few months, I watched, created a store, found the hot product, got it set up, built an Instagram page for traffic, got blog articles written & much more!

I did all that on my own.

3 months had passed by since I had that introductory Shopify meeting with Mikey.

When I made my first sale, I decide to give Mikey a call to let him know about the progress since our initial talk. He gives me a proud look & says congratulations.

2 weeks in, my friends are telling me that Mikey is telling everyone he's the only reason why I made money from the business.

The proud look he had wasn't because I won.
Rather, it was because he thought HE was the reason that I won.

He completely undermined my work.

This may not seem like direct competing to you, but it is indirect. In his mind, he sees me winning. Rather than give me props, he wants to find a way to take credit for it.

These sorts of people have **scarcity mindset.**

I've worked with a lot of people in the business world, and I want to tell you something...

You don't want scarcity minded people in your squad.

These people aren't looking out for your best interests. They are looking out for their best interests. If you win, great. But that's only an afterthought to their own wins.

A great friend views their friend's win as their own win. That's how I like to filter my squad nowadays.

This filtration system alone filters out A LOT of people. You'll be surprised by how many people have a scarcity mindset towards winning.

They think there aren't too many opportunities out there. So, they get defensive when a friend wins, because they feel like they just lost an opportunity.

It's all about investing in the right squad. In order to do that, something difficult needs to be done.

'Like?'
Assessing who you are.

When I was doing the Shopify store, I had a scarcity mindset myself. I was the guy who was always hoarding information, felt jealous when I saw someone doing better & felt like opportunities were very rare.

That's why I went onto attract the Mikey's of the world.

So, I went on a journey to level up & change my character as a whole.

After transforming myself for the last few years, I realized that the tribe I attracted was simply a projection of my

subconscious mind & my awareness of my
subconscious mind.

Are you always competing with your squad?
Is your squad always competing with you?

Well in both instances, it is your fault.
Not fair, but true.

Distance from that squad.
Now fall back & work on yourself.

Next, build one social asset at a time to build strong bonds.

Once you have built 5 strong bonds with stand up people,
then introduce them to each other in a group chat. That's the
new tribe.

Help each other level up. Have each other's backs &
celebrates each other's wins.

That's how the invisible glue strengthens & the power of the
tribe only compounds over time.

What All Cowards Have In Common

When I was 5 years old, I was pushed into the pool by my cousin. Not the shallow 3-foot side. But the deep 6-foot side.

At that time, I had no clue how to swim. Since it was a party, there were a bunch of kids in the swimming pool. So, it looked like I was swimming, while in reality, I was **drowning**.

After a while, someone was able to notice I was drowning and point it out. My dad, plus 2 other friends jumped in the water to save me. As you can tell, I did not drown.

Fast forward a few years later.

Now I am in middle school. Our gym class had swimming sessions where the swimmers were split into categories.

-Class C swimmers were the worst.
-Class B swimmers were okay.
-Class A swimmers were the best.

I was in Class A.

'Wait, what?? I thought you weren't going to swim after the drowning incident?'
That's what I thought. But no. The exact opposite happened.

After I was about to drown that day, I realized I had a huge flaw. I didn't know how to swim. It was evident that I needed to learn.

For the next few months, my dad, brother & I would go to the local pool and learn how to swim. We learned the basics & worked our way up. The more exposure I got to swimming, the easier it got. Soon, I went from treating it like a chore to racing with the other kids in the pool.

To go from the little boy who almost drowned to a Class A swimmer, was a journey. The middle portion of the transition meant **everything**.

Either learn from the experience or shift blame.

Initially, I wanted to do the latter. I hated my cousin who pushed me in the water that day. Wanted to blame him for catching me off guard. But behind that blame, I was low key embarrassed.

That embarrassment bought awareness to my flaw. Therefore, I was forced to show courage.

What do all cowards have in common?
They all shift the blame.

Seen it time & time again.

They are exposed to a massive weakness in their arsenal. Rather than take accountability & make incremental progress, they do the exact opposite. They blame someone else to preserve their ego & maintain status quo.

While their courageous counterparts **must** sting their ego.

Yes. All courageous people **must** sting their ego if they want to show courage.

Platitude time.

Courage isn't the absence of fear.
Courage is continuing despite of fear.

Cowards feel the fear & simply cannot progress forward. If
they left it at that, then it would be okay!

Because eventually, the level of guilt will cause them to take a
hard look in the mirror & possibly do something about it.

However, when you shift blame, then you officially cut of any
growth.
Finger pointers don't thrive in the real world. They fool their
brain into thinking there is no issue at all. This is a 1st degree
felony to your character.

Finger pointers are never going to be in the
battlefield creating something. They will be on the side with
their tail between their legs talking a big game. When push
comes to shove, there will only be all bark & no bite.

All flash & 0 substance.

Courage isn't sexy. It's an arduous process that requires time
& consistency.

I hated swimming at first because I had memories of
drowning with the activity. But after doing it long enough, I
ended up enjoying it. Thought it was fun.

In the level up world, we always take care of
unfinished business. Don't count yourself out of a race that is
truly a marathon.

You were the only one running this marathon all along.

O competition.

Lucid Dreaming

Words play a big role in reality.

Not sure where I heard it, but someone said, "Words are the lens for the mind."

One observation that I have noticed since writing is that my thinking has gotten clearer.

What I have noticed as of late is that my dreams have gotten clearer as well. When I wake up, I remember a lot of it.

Not all of it though. But the most I have ever in my life. I don't know if that's because of writing every day, or because I stopped using my phone for the first few hours of waking up. I invested in an alarm clock & leave my phone in another room.

It may be the prior.
It may be the latter.
It may be both.

What does lucid dreaming have to do with communication skills? A lot to be honest.

It's hard to be a clear, concise communicator if you are a messy thinker.

The mental faculties & speaking/writing skills have a seesaw like effect.

While dreaming, the mind flows without restrictions.

One thing I notice from my dreams is that it's not always about me. A lot of them still center around me. But also, a lot of the dreams center around ambiguous concepts.

Had a dream a while back about a teacher disciplining a student who was always forgetting their homework. Wasn't sure who the kid was. But my mind had created him. I was simply an observer.

Observing dreams gives a 4-D perspective of the mind. When the ego is momentarily slashed, life can be perceived from different angles.

Sort of like going from having ONLY the front windshield in your car to now having the windshield, the side mirrors & the rear-view mirror.

Understanding the mind on a deeper level builds creativity.

There are new perspectives to approach topics with. Content creation skyrockets as well.

Everyone has a different method when it comes to dreaming. I'm no expert on this by any means.

What I recommend you do is avoid reaching for the phone when you wake up.

Soon as you wake up, make it a conscious effort to recall fragments of your dream. It'll be tough, but it's doable. It's sloppy in the beginning, but it improves with time.

The process of waking up is a handover from the subconscious mind back to the conscious mind. This is the relaxed brain wave state.

Lucid dreaming gives access to a new world that we have
been sleeping on (all the pun intended).

Energy

Do you know the definition of intelligence?

'Someone who does very well in exams.'

And?

'What do you mean and? That's it. Someone who does very well in exams.'

Is that your final answer?

'Yessir.'

Well, my friend...

You are wrong.

Intelligence in the real world is the ability to acquire and apply a skill.

That is what true intelligence is about.

You can Google some definitions, sure. Or you can just evaluate your own life. Since being out there in the real world, what has really mattered?

'My skills.'

Exactly.

I want to share why I believe emotional regulation is key. Why Emotional Quotient (EQ) is true intelligence.

IQ and Energy

IQ measures mental alertness, which is great. It is an

excellent measurement for your pattern recognition skills.

So yes, in that regards, IQ is great.

But something is still missing homie.
'What is that?'
Heart.

Mental alertness is an accurate way to measure our brains ability for logical processing. This is all a part of our conscious mind aka the thinking mind. But the real world is not always fair.

Your IQ would have mattered a ton in the real world if there wasn't a thing called the human ego. The human ego makes the entire world an emotional & social atmosphere. Both components that are **illogical**.

'Wait! Really? Humans are not logical?'
No, they are not.

At their biological core, they are emotional, **not logical**, creatures.

Which is why in order to survive in the real world, you have to understand the power of energy. It is your energy that will make or break you. Your energy is far more important than your mental alertness.

Why is energy so important?

Energy is so important because your life is mainly dominated by it. You process information with your emotional brain

BEFORE your logical brain.

'Can you give me an example?'
Sure. Public speaking.

You have an intense jolt of anxiety when you think about speaking to an audience of 500 people.

Therefore, after **feeling** the emotion of fear & anxiety, you logically talk yourself out of giving the speech. You think with your logical brain second.

'Okay, I see what you mean. Mind giving one more example please?'
Sure. Picture the last time you got mad at someone.

What happened?
'I felt a STRONG physical sensation & I snapped.'
Aha!

You felt a strong emotion & reacted. How did you feel afterward?
'Shame.'
See? Your logic took the back burner to your emotions.

Bottom line is this:
Subconscious mind > Conscious mind

Emotions are your core subconscious self.
Logic is a part of your thinking conscious mind.

What is EQ?

There is no exam for your EQ. Only you know how your internal world operates. So this is a quotient that you will have to deduce for yourself. EQ will be measured by asking yourself the following:

1. How aware am I of my emotions?
2. How much understanding do I have over my emotions?
3. How well can I regulate my emotions?
4. How well am I aware of other people's emotions?

These are a few questions that I want you to ponder on. 'Okay. And by doing this, I am going to be able to learn skills better as well?'
Yes.

How EQ affects your Intelligence

Remember earlier how I mentioned intelligence was the ability to acquire & apply skills?
'Yea.'
Well, here's the thing. I have learned hard skills AND soft skills in my life. Few examples:

Hard skills: coding, circuit building, scripting
Soft skills: public speaking, storytelling

Want to know what I noticed?
'What?'
ANY skill can be learned with the following:

1. Deliberate practice
2. Consistency
3. Drive

Therefore, you can be learning for your ENTIRE life. Your goal for your entire life should be to skill build. Intelligence is not fixed due to number 3 from my list:

DRIVE.

Drive is a key component of EQ. That internal motivation? That's ALL emotional intelligence. The warriors who have the drive are the ones that will make it to the top.

No matter what field you put them in.

Engineering is "supposed" to be a field for High IQ people. No, not true.

I've seen many people who came in with 0 engineering experience. But they showed heart day in and day out. Learned all the code, circuit building, scripting (that is supposed to be all IQ dominant) and they found ways to rise up.

That's what true intelligence about.

Drive also allows you to overpower any negative emotions to keep going for the future.

What do you think matters more:

How well your pattern recognition skills are, or how much heart you show to keep pushing forward even when shit gets tough?

Bottom Line

Here is the plain fact. Your brain has **high** plasticity.
'English please?'
You can learn anything with repetition.

So quit thinking your intelligence is fixed. Our ancestors had no clue what an IQ was. They showed heart to grow and survive.

You must do the same.

From here on out, do not let any exam deter you from knowing that you can pick up any skill that you want. You simply need to show the #1 side of EQ, which is drive.

Seinfeld Challenge:

Which one do you personally think is more important for skill building, EQ or IQ? I am issuing you a challenge today.

So I want you to pick up ANY skillset you can think of. Hard skill or soft skill.

Got it?
'Yessir.'

Now do the following:
1. *Buy a calendar with all months on one page.*
2. *Buy a red sharpie.*
3. *Practice with purpose every day & mark an X on the day.*

Do not let the chain break!

Keep doing this every day. Doesn't matter if you practice the skill for only 3 minutes that day. But make sure you practice every day.

I don't care what your IQ score is. I guarantee if you show the drive to keep the chain going & the emotional intelligence to overcome your self-doubt & laziness, then you will figure the skill out.

Go ahead & test out this challenge to see for yourself!

The Power of the Inside Joke

When I was in high school, I had this Spanish teacher named Ms. Darna. She was this Cuban lady with short hair, bright lipstick & a travel bag suitcase with her.

Overall, very laid back.

She used to expect more out of me. I was in my final year of Spanish class, yet couldn't formulate a sentence.

'Armani. You let me down' she said in her thick Spanish accent.

But it wasn't just me.

A lot of the IB kids in her class struggled. A lot of the kids BESIDES this one guy named Gui.

Gui was this Brazilian fellow who was well traveled. He learned a bunch of languages growing up. So, Ms. Darna's class was light work to him.

'How come you didn't ask Gui to help you?'

It's because Gui was a loner. He would always sit by himself in class and would always stay away from everyone.

One day, a few of the IB kids realized we needed someone to tutor us. Otherwise, we may fail.

Becoming friends with Gui was starting to become a

priority.

A few of the IB kids & I had a tradition of going to an Asian Buffet after school on Tuesdays. We decided that we were going to invite Gui to build some rapport.

I went up the next Tuesday & asked Gui if he wanted to join? I was expecting him to be disinterested.

No, that was not the case.

You could tell he was waiting for someone to invite him to something. Being a loner was getting to him.

That day, it was 4 of the usuals, plus Gui going to the Asian buffet. We had no clue how this was going to go.

As we sat down, we began talking...but Gui remained quiet.

We talked about sports... Gui didn't say a word.

We talked about girls... Gui didn't say a word.

We talked about the food... Gui didn't say a word.

What the hell? This dude was boring as shit. How were we supposed to become friends with this?? Give us something to work with champ.

As we were brainstorming on what to say next, one of us made a very stunning observation.

Our plates.

When you go to a buffet, what does your plate look like? 'It is filled with food.'

Exactly. For me & the usuals, our plates were full.

But for Gui? It was almost empty. It wasn't fully empty though.

He had some Orange chicken stacked on the side.

Some Beijing beef on the other side.

A tad bit of noodles.

With lettuce sprinkled on top.

Overall, his plate was **very** organized.

At that point, one of the kids from our squad named Asif pointed out how 'fancy' Gui's plate looked.

The rest of us noticed & busted out laughing.

Asif was like:
'From here on out, Gui's nickname is Fancy Boy.'

At that point, Gui started to join in on the laughter as well.

'Nah guys, I'm not fancy like that' he said.

But he said it in a way where you could tell he liked his new nickname.

Officially, an inside joke was born.

The next day when we saw Gui, the squad and I went up to him and was like: 'Yo Fancy boy, come sit with us.'

Gui was down. He was no longer a loner.

This was a mutualistic relationship for all parties involved.

Gui finally had friends. And we ended up learning a little bit of Spanish. Enough to pass Ms. Darna's quizzes.

Around that time, I was able to learn the value of an inside joke.

Other kids in the class would be like, *'Why do y'all keep calling Gui Fancy Boy?'*

But we would never say. It wouldn't be an inside joke if everyone knew.

That's what some weasels don't understand. A weasel is someone who violates the unwritten rules of friendship. They spill inside jokes to outsiders.

Spilling an inside joke takes out the magic. Also, when you make the same inside joke with multiple people, it can also take out the magic.

Till graduating high school, Gui was known as Fancy Boy among the squad. Many others kept getting curious. However, we would never say. Not even Gui.

All the friends have gone our own ways. I only know a handful of people now that I knew in high school. Yet, the memory still is remembered.

Inside jokes are powerful.

When you build a social bond, inside jokes can emerge. Nothing that you have to PLAN out too much. There's no fun in that.

With Gui & the squad, it just happened from an authentic interaction.

Inside jokes work within any type of social interaction. No discrimination.

Why is it powerful?

Because these jokes build trust among the parties involved. People like getting exclusive information.

Also, it builds an Us vs. Them sort of mentality.
Not the violent Us vs. Them.
Rather, a very lighthearted one.

A great joke is one that is easy to remember. Reiterating it is what allows it to stick.

Powerful social dynamics are not taught in school. Just taught in the school of hard knocks.

Ðark Charisma

Alfred Nobel was a peaceful man. When we think of the Nobel peace prize, we think of a peaceful award.

However, what we may not know about Alfred Nobel is that he holds the patent for the dynamite. When we think of a dynamite, the last thing we think of is peaceful.

Alfred didn't make the dynamite for malicious reasons. He thought this invention could help the world. He was shocked when he saw his precious invention being used for such destruction.

In my eyes, charisma is the dynamite of the social world. It can be used for a lot of good and it can be used for a lot of evil.

Street smarts is where everyone has a chance to show what they are about. It doesn't matter if someone is 6'8, a man, a woman, a certain religion etc.

There are no rules.

Which opens the playing field for everyone.

'You're telling me ugly people can be charismatic too?'
Yes.

Don't confuse handsome with being attractive. Handsome is physical attributes. Attractive is behavioral attributes.

I knew this pudgy short kid name Jimmy. He **thought** he was muscular.

You could tell his looks meant a lot to him. He'd always suck his gut in and do his best to dress up.

Jimmy knew how to make you feel like a celebrity. Full focus when you're talking. Asking all the right questions and telling all the funny jokes.

Even though Jimmy looked like a ninja turtle, it was commonly accepted that he was a charismatic person. Surprisingly, he ended up getting a lot of girls too while being the short guy.

'That seems great man! Jimmy seems like a cool guy.'
However, that was the problem.

Jimmy was a dictionary definition of a snake.

He's one of those snakes that breaks guy code. He'd often gossip about guys to women.

When you are around him, he seems like one of the boys. But deep inside, he was just taking intel to share it with the girls.

The Gaslight Effect is an example of dark charisma.

This is when someone shows a lot of attention in a profound way in the beginning of a relationship. And then can take it away out of the blue moon. A dark charisma move.

How do you spot sinister social moves?

It's not easy to spot because these humans are very good at social skills. Which is why it's smart to fight fire with fire.

o   Fighting fire with fire is fighting charisma with charisma.

The people who can see through dark charisma are the people with light charisma. Light charisma is how we PERCEIVE charisma should be used in the first place.

Light charisma is built through a simple fundamental concept. Straying away from this concept leads to confusion. Stay with this concept & light charisma follows.
Here it goes:
Leave others better off than you found them.

Leaving others better off than you found them is the advancing personality that Wallace Wattles brings up in his book, Science of Getting Rich.
A lot of principles of wealth can be applied to people skills.

People with light charisma build a strong level of street smarts. So, they can tell when someone is trying to dupe them.

Unfortunately, a 100% success rate is not a reality in the world of people. Even the brightest of light charisma may get bit by a dark charisma individual every now and then.

Yet, nothing in this world is 100%.
That's an illusion.

Charisma is not a finite state that is figured out and never worked on again. Instead, it's a lifelong activity.

It's a game of being more aware of your surroundings, understand your feelings, and learning to listen.
Feelings are especially important because charisma comes

down to SUBJECTIVE science.

Science which is based off experiences. Feelings are raw energy that is meant to be perceived by you. Feelings are nature's whispers when you fix your ears.

Listening will help you out a lot too. Not where you are just nodding your head like a dummy.

But when your mind is turning their words into pictures in your imagination.

Learn your feelings, listen more and you'll be more aware of your surroundings.

Repeat this.

If you are a good person, then light charisma will evolve in you.

Being a Problem Solver

One of the beauties about social media is that it allows you to be creative. One of the bad parts of social media is that it allows you to be creative.

I used to use my personal Twitter account a lot.
This is a place where I follow sports pages, entertainment & some friends.

When I used to predominantly use that Twitter, I HATED it.
'Haha, why?'
Because it was so damn negative.

I checked it recently because my friend said he sent me a message there.
When I checked, I realized somethings never change.

It was just an endless stream of doom and gloom. If that's the only side of Twitter you knew, then you would think the world would be ending any second.

That's the thing with the masses. They undermine the great era that we are living in to focus on everything that is going wrong.

Yes, the world does have things going wrong with it. Denying that would be silly. Any stage in human history has things going wrong with it though.

Things going wrong are just a part of mother nature.

When I check this side of doom and gloom twitter, I notice 4 girls who stick out.

These were girls I knew in college. Super quiet and meek when you see them in person. Need to tilt your head close to hear them speaking.

But on Twitter?
Straight loudmouth, negative, toxic creatures.

They write in all caps, keep talking about how bad men are & how bad their culture is. Not all the girls I follow.

Just these 4.

When I look at it, I realize that this is a good thing. Twitter gives you access to someone's mind.
When someone behaves like that on social media, you know how they are like when the mask is off.

I don't say this to demean these 4 girls. But I understand why they behave like this.
'Why?'
Because they are problem finders. The problem though is that they are not FINISHING the job.

A good problem solver is a problem finder & a solver.

If they can't solve it, then they go on a journey to solve it. That's what sparks learning in the first place.

These 4 girls just get on Twitter, talk shit & then go back to their privileged lives. Pretty comical.

What's hilarious is that they think they have it tough. But they don't. They need to be placed in the hood or the villages for a couple of weeks to learn how to be humble. But that's not a realistic situation.

So, you just want to use these 4 girls as a lesson of what NOT to be.

The reason I recommend problem finding AND problem solving is that finding begins the journey of solving.

That's how entrepreneurs, engineers & innovators are born.

Don't be blind to the problems of the world. Acknowledge it. Develop a level of sensitivity to it so you enhance your awareness.

However, after you find the problems, don't just bitch about it on twitter. If you do, at least aim to propose a solution too.

Problem - Solution = Whining
Problem + Solution = Potential Business Idea

'How do I solve the problem though?'
With creativity.

There is no 1 way to solve a problem. Finding the problem is the second hardest part.
'Then what's the *first* hardest part?'
Finding the resources to get the issue resolved.

How you get the resources is on you.
-Sometimes, it will be via experiences.
-Other times, it will be via advice.

-Other times, it will be asking strategic questions to the internet.

A problem is not going to get solved by being outraged & mailing it in. That's a loser's mindset. A winner's mindset is finishing the job.

Small acts can turn into character traits really quick.

I knew these 4 girls in undergrad, and they seemed like they would whine here and there on their tweets.

Now it's their only subject matter.
Pretty sad when you think about it.

By solving one big problem, you solve a lot of micro problems along the way. That's why no one can fully teach you how to fully solve a problem.

That's like someone teaching you how to talk in a conversation. Can they do it? Sure. But telling you what to say makes you dependent rather than independent.

Sort of like those movies where there is a smooth-talking guy talking in a microphone to the ear of a loser who is on a date. The loser is not learning diddly squat.
Just reciting like a dummy.

Solve your problems by knowing that you can.

You've had 5 moments in your life where you thought you dug the hole too deep. Yet, creativity had your back.

We all have those 5 moments.

If the problem means enough...
You will solve it.
And that we will.

Story of the Funniest YouTuber

A couple of years ago, I was in Las Vegas.
There was a moment where I saw a few people asking this guy for an autograph.

It was a little guy with a backwards cap, white, earrings etc.
Seemed like a normal guy.

Is he some kind of celebrity? I wondered.
The people I was with had no clue who he was.

Once the group was done taking pics with the guy, I went up to one of them & asked them who he was. They looked surprised that I didn't know the mystery guy.

'You don't know who that is?? That's Vincent Valentine!' they said.
said.
Who??

After some time, they told me that he was a famous YouTuber who pranked people in Las Vegas. He was popular in the local area and his channel was blowing up!

Once I got back to Florida, I checked out his channel.

The dude was hilarious.

Not regular hilarious. To me, he was the funniest pranking channels that I ever came across.

I've seen other prank channels. Vitaly, Fousey, Hood Pranks etc. Those were cool. However, something about them did not feel right.

With Vincent Valentine? He felt like the real deal. Ultra-composed, timely humor & seems like your friend.

His YouTube channel name was Limitless EXP.

After watching a few of his videos, I was surprised by the latest post.
This post was made in 2016.
Where he said he was quitting YouTube.

Huh?? I thought you were just getting started...
Damn.

After going through the video, I could sense what the issue was.
He was starting to get a lot of negative comments on his videos.

The negative comments came from the freeloaders who were whining & asking for more videos. Or just whining in general.

Vincent Valentine had more fans. But unfortunately, the negativity bias often hears the criticisms first & the loudest.

What could have been a great YouTuber unfortunately does not make videos anymore.
Still, to this day, I view him as the funniest prank channel out.

There's some hope that he makes a comeback. Who knows?

Guy is super young.

What were a few of the lessons?
Plenty, now that I think about it.

The most important part is that it's better to attract your true tribe over numbers.

Doubt Vincent wanted his channel to blow up to the extent that it did.

More people is not always a good thing.

Honestly, more people lead to more freeloaders.
Human nature isn't always pretty.

It's better to have 1000 true fans than 1,000,000 iffy people who only ask and never give.

The tough part is that the brain focuses on the negatives over the positives if you let it.

That's why you need to take CONSCIOUS effort to keep the vision targeted, clear & to the point.
Otherwise, the mind treats the negative opinions like the Velcro.

'What's your tip for this issue if you were in his position?'
I think the best tip is to talk to one person no matter how big your audience gets.

Talk to your younger self rather than a target market.

This may have confused some people.

But try it. Create for your younger self...Forget the market research for a few.

What you will notice is that the content your younger self needed resonates with a lot of people's present-day self.

And just like that, you are ATTRACTING a market rather than seeking it.

The story of Vincent Valentine is powerful.
Something tells me that he may one day make a return.

Hopefully once he's back, it's back to the roots.
Back to focusing on the younger self.

The younger self is what attracts the 1000 true fans. Forget the millions.

Dry Humor

A couple of years back, I was at a work social and was talking to one of my coworkers. His name was Justin.

As I am talking to this guy, one of the workers from my floor came to me. His name was Glen.

Justin was this Asian guy around my age. We were both 25 at the time. Glen was a guy in his 40s. He was a position or two higher than us.

Well, Glen comes up to me & starts creating conversation.

Just for a little context, Glen has a lot of dark humor. It's like you need to know him to find him funny.
Otherwise, you may not find him funny...

Not only will you not find him funny. You may perceive him as disrespectful.

Glen starts cracking jokes about what I am eating. I was eating cheese cubes that the company was serving.

Then Glen looks at Justin and was like:
'Damn man, can your pants get any tighter? Looks like they were painted on you.'

Justin responds back with:
'Bold words from Humpty Dumpty.'

Then the 2 go back and forth.

I know Glen is not the guy to let someone have the last word.
And I know Justin is the same.

As they are going back & forth, I'm just standing there eating
my cheese... I'm laughing my ass off too.

I had no clue that Glen & Justin knew each other.

As it's getting really heated, I eventually bud in.
'Alright guys, chill...'
Then Glen is like to me, 'damn man, what's this guy's name?'

Wait a minute...
Y'all been going back & forth for this long & you 2 don't even
know each other??

That was a very odd moment for me.
I've had roast offs with my *friends* before. But this was the
first time I saw 2 *strangers* talking like that with one another.

After finding out that they didn't know each other, this made
the entire situation even more funny.

I didn't know if there was anything to learn from this...
However, I did think about something:
What if it had gone left?

That wouldn't be a stretch either. Glen was a guy in his 40s
who would routinely say that he felt like he made a bunch of
poor life choices.

He had 0 desire to be in that company. So, he would
routinely let others be aware of his poor personality.

Justin was a young gun in the company. But he was building
a business on the side. The business was his passion.

He showed 0 respect to someone who was his senior if they
didn't show respect to him as well.
Ass kissing was not in Justin's rulebook.

**I really do wonder how far that heated moment would
have gone?**

The point being: dry humor is polarizing.
I like to call it sarcasm.

Humor has different tiers. One of the tier's includes laughing
at the expense of someone.
That's roasting.

Other types of humor can be self-depreciating.
Where you tell an embarrassing moment from your life.

And other comedy forms are the type of humor that you can
never tell is humor in the first place. That's sarcasm.

That's what makes it so polarizing.

I'm not a big fan of sarcasm.
But I know people who are.

When I went to my brother's wedding reception in Philly a
couple of years back, I noticed how all the Uber drivers were
sarcastic.

Yo, are you James the Uber driver?

'No, I'm Pablo Picasso.'
me standing there looking confused
'Yea man, I'm your Uber driver.'

This is how they acted.

Dry humor can be hilarious for a certain segment of the population. It's funny when one person with dry humor comes in contact with another person with dry humor.

To the outside, it looks like these 2 individuals are bickering. While in the inside, these 2 are building rapport.

Maybe that's what was going on with Justin & Glen. Maybe I perceived it as them getting heated because I am not a fan of sarcasm.

However, from their end, it was 2 people with dry humor feeling each other out.

People with dry humor exist in the social world.
They seem rude at first. But eventually, they may come to grow on you.

The whole phrase: *'he's a nice guy when you get to know him.'*
Really means: *'he has dry humor, but you just get used to it. '*

Who Wants to Be a Millionaire?

The show Who Wants to be a Millionaire, was lit. I don't know if the show is still going on. Nevertheless, I **vividly** remember how I used to watch it growing up.

It would be a thrill to answer the questions correctly. When I'd answer the question incorrectly, I'd conveniently take a restroom break.

The good ole days.

Well, I came to find out that they had a Who Wants to Be a Millionaire show in England as well.

I wasn't surprised. It was easy to see this show becoming a movement.

It had the recipe to be a success:
-People learned.
-The host was always humorous.
-The episodes would often be a thriller.

I came to learn of this man named Charles Ingram. Oh yes, the infamous Charles Ingram.

He was known as the guy who pulled off the biggest scam in television history.
Yep, he cheated on the show.

The plan consisted of him, his wife & this other fellow named
Tecwen Whittock.
This happened around 2001.

Charles's wife had been on the show earlier.
She won 32,000$.

Her brother was on the show as well.
He won 32,000$.

When Charles Ingram came on, there was this question on
whether or not he would break the 32,000$ mark.
'Well, did he??'
Yes.

He ended up winning the million.
But in an unethical way.

There was this man named Tecwen Whittock who had been
sitting in a nearby seat. And he would keep on coughing for
the right answers.

It was truly stunning to watch.
Especially when you know they were eventually caught.

In the show, Charles Ingram would keep reciting each answer
out loud. Waiting to hear the cough.

His wife was in on it too. Coughing occasionally on the right
answer.

The plan was brilliant when you thought about it. How could
anyone tell? These were subtle coughs to say the least.

Charles got his million.
He broke the 32,000$ curse.

But did he really break anything?
No.

After some time, he was caught.
This was very dark news for the squad.

'How bad are we talking?'
Well, there is a documentary talking about the grandest scam
in television history. It's called "Major Fraud."

Just like that, Charles, his wife, & Tecwen Whittock's lives had
a giant black mark. They were labeled cheaters by their
community.

What I found very peculiar about this story is the level of
genius they already had and how they poorly squandered it.

Because let's think about this for a second.
Let's say you win the million.

Then, I'm assuming you have to pay a significant amount for
taxes. I doubt you keep the entire million. This is me just
guessing.

Let's say you hypothetically walk away with 850,000$. They
all divide it up to 3. That's around 283,000$ for each of
them.

Now it begs the question, *was it worth it?*

Nothing about 283,000$ seems so staggering to potentially

throw my life away. The money will be given, yes. But then there's always that feeling of looking behind my back.

That's why I never understood people who robbed banks. Like what are you really expecting from all of this?

You get some dollars.

But most likely, you will get caught. Especially with the advancement of technology nowadays.
Was the money worth always looking behind your back?

The reason that this situation was very peculiar was due to the guy named Tecwen Whittock.
He was apparently a teacher.

A guy with that intellect making such poor judgment shows that anyone can fall victim to greed. A momentary lapse in judgment can make something like this happen.

This is why ethical business practices are slowly starting to make a comeback.

Also, this is why the process needs to consistently be valued as much as the results.
Both are needed.

When I see debates of systems vs goals, it shows shortsightedness in perspective. Both are joined at the hip.

A system is only a system when the moving parts are working towards a goal. Otherwise, you just have a bunch of moving parts. Plus, a goal is a system manifested.

When the mind just focuses on one, and completely excludes the other, that's when poor judgment happens.

Also, I believe this is another reason why a big part of social skills is knowing when **not** to be social. Knowing how not to talk to people is just as important as knowing how to talk to people.

Each human invited leads to potential chaos.
Just need to decide which chaos is worth it.

I don't know who hatched this brilliant plan of cheating the million dollars. What's done is done.

Charles was able to put it behind him. Heck, him & his wife showed up in the celebrity couple's edition of the other TV show, the Weakest Link.

It's great not to kick someone while they are down. However, it's even better to learn the lessons.

Personalize the lessons.

So the subconscious knows that the process leading to the goal was set up like that for a reason.

Skipping the process is bad karma.

It feels good momentarily.
But when it comes crashing down...
It really does come crashing down.

Motivation That Lasts

It's easy to get carried away. Especially when a movement becomes popularized. Self-improvement is no different.

Self-improvement has several of punch lines. Some that constitute as meaningful information. Other punch lines are seen as a mockery.

One of those punchlines:
'It is not motivation that will do the trick, it is discipline!'

Although I agree with a huge portion of that statement, it is sort of misleading. Discipline will help you get there. But discipline mixed with the right motivation will help you get there AND have fun.

There are 2 kinds of motivation:

1. Motivation that does not last.
2. Motivation that does last.

For group 1, picture the people who begin the year off with a bunch of New Year's resolutions.

They are going to get in shape.

They are going to stay committed to their diet.

They are going to start that business that they've been delaying.

So, they begin the year off with a bunch of enthusiasm for the

task. They work & hustle away. Day in & day out,
their motivation has them feeling pumped.

But as a few weeks go by? That motivation begins to melt
away.

They realize that the beginning portion of any venture is the
hardest part. They didn't plan for the roadblocks along the
way, so when they face them, they get discouraged.

They get so discouraged that after hitting a few roadblocks,
they decide to quit. Tsk tsk.

Don't believe me? Compare January 2nd of the gym to March
2nd.

There is a massive difference.

The reason that this group quit was because their **intention**
was wrong from the get-go.

Ask them why they are doing what they are doing & they
typically will give a shallow answer or no answer at all!

They will say they were doing it for adoration, to prove
someone wrong or just because they were bored.

Due to a lack of a strong foundational WHY fueling the
moves, this person quit when the going got tough.

However, for the motivation that *lasts*?
Different.

The motivation that lasts requires a 2-part process: The Push
& Pull.

It's a combination of fear & pleasure.

Push: Runaway

In this step, the person is running away from something that terrifies them. Back to the gym example. What are some terrifying scenarios?

Obesity, a heart attack, not living long enough to see your family etc.

Pull: Run towards

In this step, the person is running towards something that will create joy in them.

A 6 pack, more stamina, fitting into your old clothes etc.

A combination of both emotions unleashes a fire that radiates. Not one that dims when the going gets tough.

I am afraid of mediocrity & hopeful for success. I never work, I just do what I was born to do. That's how emotions fuel discipline.

Push & pull.

Motivation that lasts adds color to a lifeless routine & turns discipline into ecstasy.

You Become What You Consume

You ever heard the old saying, you are what you eat?

'Yes. Why?'

Because there is another version of that.

'What is that?'

You become what you consume.

I am not joking. You know the stuff that you are watching, reading & taking in? ALL of those will come back to shape your future.

This is a big deal. You may be negatively rewiring your subconscious mind and not have a clue.

Your mind is your best friend in this cruel, volatile world and you need it by your side.

Let me tell you a story when I learned about the consumption concept the hard way.

I want to tell you a story about the 2016 election.

Obama stepping down, what's next?

I'll be honest, I was never into politics like that.

But 2015 was a little bit more different.

'Why?'

I wanted to see what the hype with politics was all about.

President Obama was wrapping up his presidential term within the next year. Who was going to be next?

This year seemed much more different than any prior political years. There seemed to be a lot more hype behind this upcoming election.

There were tons of people from my friend circle bringing up politics nonstop.

'Why do you think that was?'
Well, for a few reasons. One part was the fact that Hillary Clinton was running again.

If she had won, she would be the nation's first woman president. Around 2015, everyone thought she would easily clobber Bernie Sanders to become the Democratic candidate.

But with the Republican side?
There were tons of people running, I believe 15 people at least. But what really got the buzz started was Donald Trump running for president.

I knew Donald Trump as the businessman who did the Apprentice. Now he was running for president?
That was out of left field.

And guess what?
The mainstream media picked up on that!

Within the next few months, the early campaigning had begun.

Few Months in

Few months into the political process, stuff already began getting hectic.
'Hectic how?'
Well, everything seemed hostile. The presidential candidates were all name calling, the media was name calling & the people around the US were name calling.

Everything seemed so damn heated.

I barely had a clue on what policies these candidates even stood for. All I knew was the latest insult that one had thought of for the other. Something seemed a little spooky.

How come we are only being shown all this controversial stuff?

I get it, all presidential elections become hectic. But why weren't we being shown anything about these people's policies?

I thought I would get back into politics for this 2016 election, but immediately noticed something bizarre.

'What?'
Literally, if you turned on any of the mainstream media channels, ALL they talked about was Donald Trump.
I was stunned to be quite honest.

At first, I thought the media would be showing this sort of coverage as the election got started. But not quite.

Each of the mainstream channels were just showing bits &
clips of controversial clips. That's it.

Trump was not the only one getting mauled by the media.
Hilary Clinton was getting slaughtered for her entire server
issue and how she handled that entire situation.

It seemed like we were being more informed on the scandals
& everything that was wrong rather than a lick of policy that
you know... can affect our lives.

At that point, something seemed off. I wanted to stay
informed this year, but how was I going to do that?
All I was hearing was a whole lot of gossip that seemed like
hot air.

At a certain point, I began to get fed up!

You know what? Fuck it. I am just going to go back to a life
without politics, this seems draining.

Something very creepy was happening as the elections were
playing out.
'What?'

Chaos arises

The ongoing negative coverage of both leading candidates
came with massive consequences.
'Such as?'
It seemed like anytime I would turn on FOX, MSNBC, CNN etc.
there were just a dump of negative energy.

Well, all that negative energy began to change some personalities.

A few of my sweetest, kind-hearted friends were getting in screaming contests with other people about political issues.

People were hurling out the terms like "racist", "liar", "corrupt" so nonchalantly.

Every time I would go out with my friends, the night would become polluted when someone would bring up politics. My friends began to notice that I would take the backburner when politics were being discussed.

And you know what would happen?
'What?'
They got mad at me!

My friends were upset that I was not half as outraged as they were about everything that was 'going on.'

'Armani, you need to start taking politics more seriously. The world has chaos all over it right now. You need to become more aware.'

I was stunned, considering that the world had seemed good to me. Well, let me clarify, there were a lot of tragedies going on around the planet for sure.

But in terms of politics, I will be 100% real. None of that shit was helping me become a better version of myself. If it wasn't helping me level up, then I considered it a waste of my damn time.

My friends had different plans for me. They would all begin
droning on & on about why Trump was a racist & Clinton
was a crook.

'Damn, that's pretty stunning stuff.'
No, want to know what was really stunning?
'What can be more stunning than that?'
The changed subconscious minds.

Victor to victim?

At this point in my life, I had the opportunity to see tons of
people blossom from victims to victors.

However, for this election cycle?
Exact opposite.

People who were victors for years were slowly becoming
victims.
'Wait, what do you mean? Is that even possible?'

Well, one of my boys, Tommy, was this e-commerce
superstar. He found 2 winning products on AliExpress &
managed to build a few Shopify stores for it. His stores were
mega successful! He was pulling in 5 figures of revenue a
month and was hitting 30% margins.

Solid stuff.

He inspired me so much that I had also started getting into e-
commerce as well. Working on my first e-commerce store
was one of the main reasons I distanced myself from politics

in the first place.

However, Tommy was beginning to change...

Initially, Tommy and I would talk nonstop about our business & how we were going to make some major moves. But now?

Tommy was always whining about how the world would be over any second.

'If Trump wins, we are screwed. If Hilary wins, we are screwed. I am so scared! My life is going to be so tough after this' Tommy would say.

What are you talking about dude? Why do you sound so fucking defeated nowadays?

'Armani, I am not being defeated. Why even bother keeping my Shopify stores running if the world is doomed?'

I was stunned to witness what I was hearing.

Tommy was literally talking like a self-defeated loser. What happened to the winner that inspired me to bring the best out in myself? Where was the old Tommy who talked me through the dark times of launching my store to help me keep pushing forward.
Where was that warrior?

The sad truth was, he wasn't there. Something in him had changed, and he did not even know it.

'What happened?'
Subconscious rewiring happened. Tommy went from a

warrior to a worrier.

I have been learning psychology for years. For most of my
early life, I was a loser who had 0 confidence.
In order to rebuild the life that I wanted, I had to learn
psychology & see how I could reprogram myself.

'Well, what did you learn?'
I learned that it is never too late to change for the best.
Neuroscience proves that our brain has a high level of
plasticity. But you know what Tommy taught me?
'What?'
It is never too late to change for the worst.

You become what you consume.

The 2016 election was a very scary thing to witness
firsthand. I saw stories being sensationalized for ratings that
were polluted with straight up venom.
All the garbage that the mainstream media was pushing was
being fed as 'news' to the average bubbas.

People who watched that content religiously did their
subconscious mind a huge disservice.

'What does the subconscious mind have to do with the *you
become what you consume* theory?'
I'll share what it has to do with it.

The Mind Rewiring.

The conscious mind is responsible for day-to-day thinking.

This is the mind that you are using to read this piece of text right now. Think of it as your thinking mind.

However, the subconscious mind is much more powerful. Your subconscious mind has data of every single memory since your childhood.

When you meditate, you will often have times when a memory from your childhood pops up. That's the subconscious mind.

Point being, the subconscious mind does not sleep.
It's stays awake and is always listening.
'What if I have something playing in the background & am not paying attention?'
Incorrect thought process.

Your conscious mind is not paying attention.
But your subconscious mind is absorbing it.

Your subconscious mind does not only feed off of TV shows. It is always aware of its surroundings. When I was hanging out with Tommy & all my negative friends who were obsessing over politics, I felt more drained.

And remember!
The conscious mind gets all its data from the subconscious mind. The conscious mind is what you are aware of as your current reality.

Your next steps

Right now, I am going to share more of what *not* to do.

1. Watch out for what you are watching. That isn't to say that you can't watch the occasional horror movie. I'll be honest, one of my guilty pleasures is sometimes watching funny prank videos on YouTube. But remember, repeated exposure to anything becomes your way of thinking & doing.

2. Audit your friend circle. This part is so damn important. Seriously, negative toxic friends will drain your conscious AND subconscious mind.
All this for what?
You are literally giving someone your time to get a headache in return.

3. Avoid giving into impulses. You ever had that moment when the person in front of you was driving slow as hell? And boom, an impulse shoots in your body and you become a primal savage and go into road rage mode?

Well, anytime you give in to an impulse like that in a negative manner, you condition a pattern to your subconscious mind.

Controlling what you watch, who you hang out with & your impulses will be enough to keep your subconscious mind healthy. This is the detox phase.
'What's next?'
You replace all that with good stuff!

Round 2

1. Consume empowering content. This can be following the right people on social media, reading articles, podcasts etc.

Just make sure it is helping your mind grow.

2. Find people who match your energy. Notice I did not say find 'nice' people. You can have people who match your energy who criticize you and tell you like it is. Because remember, you do not want friends head nodding. Focus all on the energy. Do you feel energized around them or not?

3. Every time you resist the temptation to fight off a dangerous impulse or emotion, then you have rewired your subconscious mind for the best! Keep fighting off these impulses & your skin will toughen.

The rest is up to you

The one thing that the 2016 election taught me was how volatile the human mind is with repetitive exposure.

You are the energy that you surround yourself with.
You become what you consume.

Consuming garbage will have you living a mediocre life really quick. It's subtle poison. What starts off as a rating grab turns into mind warping 101.

Be aware of your surroundings. Because even if your conscious mind is off in lala land, your subconscious mind is always watching.

Play for the Long Run

It's pretty funny. People love to ignore the intangible & just focus on the tangible.

Think about it.

Why do you work out the body & not the mind?
'No clue.'
It's because you can physically SEE & TOUCH the body. You cannot do either with the mind.

The brain loves structure. Without structure, it tends to throw your mind in a disarray.

A frazzled mind leads to frazzled behaviors.

Your intangible self will play a greater role on your reality than you can imagine. The spirit, mind & ego can be assets or liabilities.

But it can't be both.

The intangible element that I want to talk about is the mind.

You see how everyone gets offended by everything nowadays? It is because they have a weak mind.

They lack mental toughness.

Lacking mental toughness will make a quitter out of you.

I used to quit a lot.

Would begin something, do it a *few* times, *fail* & jump onto
the next thing. Therefore, I know exactly how quitters think.

The life cycle of a quitter:

1. They see something in the external world that
motivates them.
2. They feel super motivated, so they begin.
3a. After a series of fails, they become deflated.
3b. After a series of wins, they hit plateaus & become deflated.
4. Quit.

Sound familiar?
I bet it does.

90% + of success is going to come down to JUST SHOWING
UP.

When you show up day in & day out, your
subconscious mind starts to familiarize itself with the task,
environment, or future goal.

As it's starting to familiarize, it is going to feel a little startled.

Remember, the subconscious mind LOVES patterns. Chasing a
big goal disrupts those patterns. So yes, there will be a lot of
discomfort in the beginning stages.

At this point, most will quit. Because they FEEL bad. But a *few*
winners, I estimate 1 out of 10, will show mental resiliency.

They will continue to show up.
Day in and day out.

As the days pile up, their mind is starting to familiarize itself with these FEELINGS.

At first, those feelings scared the mind. But now?

The mind simply realizes those feelings are harmless.
Day in and day out.

Over time, the subconscious mind has formed new patterns. It sees the goal, has adjusted to the new environment & re-calibrates. You have shown mental toughness & heart.

Before entering any goal, just know that you will face challenges & plateaus.

Challenges hurt because you think you will never figure it out.

Plateaus sting because you were just figuring it out & begin to question if you broke something?

No…
Just keep showing up.

Visibility is a superpower.

Whether it's in networking, goal chasing or just building mental resiliency. Winners are eventually seen.

It's because they know they have a job to get done. And they will use their mind to overpower any uncomfortable feelings that say otherwise.

The temporary hurt will one day melt away.
The strong mind will last you for another 10 lifetimes.

A winner **always** play for the long run.

28th Birthday

I appreciate all the birthday wishes from everyone. Last year on my birthday, I released a thread call '27 Lessons' which ended up going viral.

This year, I wanted to tell a story.

When I was 16 years old, I had to prepare to take the SATs. Your boy was nervous.

I was an unbelievably bad test taker. Apparently, this exam was going to play a big role in my future.

For the next few months, I grinded away. Studied day in and day out. Got a few of those SAT books and did all the practice problems. Even enrolled in a SAT class.

As the months quickly faded, the big moment had finally arrived.

The test day was here.

A part of me was confident considering how much preparation I had done. The other part of me was unsure, not knowing what to expect....

The minute that the exam started, I noticed something.

'What was that?'
I knew it was going to be a LONG ride. The questions looked WAY harder than what I expected.

After leaving the exam, I no longer felt confident. It

completely caught me off guard.

When we got our scores back, my results reflected my worries.

I bombed the exam.

The next day, everyone in my IB program was talking about how well they did. When I told them what I got...everyone laughed.

I got the lowest SAT score in my entire class and it wasn't even close. They all scored a minimum of 250 points higher than me.

No clue what happened. I gave it my all, but I came up short.

It was back to the drawing board. Time to study again & hopefully salvage this travesty.

Another few months passes by & this time I'm ready for round 2.

I open the exam & feel much more confident. But we just need to wait and see what happens.

When I got the exam score back in the next few weeks, once again...

I scored the lowest in my class.

During that time, I didn't know why it was playing out like this. No clue why I worked so hard & these other people were scoring higher.

These kids from my class were actually bragging how they

didn't '*study at all.*'

So, what gives?

My entire life, I thought people with work ethic got ahead.
Why wasn't this the case with me?

'Did you ever find out why?'
Yea.
'And why was that?'
**Because work ethic is shown during moments of
uncertainty.**

It's been over a decade since I took the SAT exam. What's
funny is that a lot of the people who just 'winged the exam,'
have little to show for it in their present day.

Majoring in majors they hate.

Scraping by with mediocrity.

Bitching on Facebook about things they can't control.

etc.

They never learned work ethic.
They took the small things for granted.

As a decade has passed, I'd like to tell my 16-year-old self
something.

'Which is?'
That being a poor test taker would be the best thing that
would ever happen to you.
'Huh???'
Let me explain.

Doing so bad in those exams forced me to work harder. The first time when I bombed the SATs, I decided to keep on pushing.

It was work ethic through uncertainty.

The second time I bombed the SATs, once again, I kept on pushing.

It was work ethic through uncertainty.

The thing about work ethic through uncertainty is that it makes very minimal sense in your present moment. But it makes all the sense in the world in the future.

Failing those exams made me work harder. But more importantly, it allowed me to have a high threshold towards dealing with chaos.

I was never given anything in the communication skills world. Everything was learned through putting myself out there & hoping that I figure it out.

Everything was earned.

Those cats that were passing their exams with 0 work, can thrive in a structured school setting. But they are soft in the real world. They aren't remotely scrappy & throw in the towel when things get tough.

As 28 rises, I know the world is very chaotic. Random shit happens all the time. Humans are unpredictable. One minute they are your friend. The next moment, they are a snake.

But one thing that you can always rely on is being
disciplined & letting the cards fall how they may.

When the dust settles, only time will tell who was putting in
work & who was just talking.

We have yet to see.

I appreciate all the wishes.
But the best is yet to come.

Do We Live in a Virtual Reality?

There are so many different belief systems out there.I used to wonder why?

There's a simple reality. Why follow so many stories? Just live life & call it a day.

'So how come you don't think like that anymore?'
Life happened.

As I started growing up, I went through different experiences. And I needed a direction for my thoughts to flow.

One of the biggest belief systems going on around nowadays is that we live in a virtual reality.

That consciousness is a mega information system & that people are all units of consciousness playing life through avatars.

When I first heard this, I laughed.
Grown up people believe this? Ha!

It seemed like I had taken a blast to the past.

Telling stories to make sense of life.

However, it caught my eye when I saw respectable physicists and engineers talking about this.

My cousin had sent me a video on WhatsApp of him and his dad in London watching one of my YouTube videos.

'It's great seeing you cuz' he wrote.

As I watched this video of them watching one of my videos, I noticed something. The person that they were watching was not me.

It was simply a digital me.

My camera turned my analog self into a digital self. What they were seeing were pixels & compressed audio of what looks and sounds like my voice.

Yet, it wasn't me.

This is important because what seems real isn't always real.

Life is experienced through the 5 senses. The 5 senses pick up data from the external world. That data from the external world is converted into signals in the nervous system and then an experience is experienced.

From the grand scheme of things, only a FRACTION of the electromagnetic spectrum is visible to humans. The rest is up for grabs.

I got my master's in information systems. On my final year, I ended up writing a research paper on virtual reality & augmented reality.

It's ironic, because in the paper, I posed whether or not we live in a virtual reality. My professor said it was an interesting question. Most masters professors are super chill and just encourage you to be curious. I completely forgot about that research paper and even posing that question.

'What's the difference between augmented reality & virtual reality?'
Augmented reality leverages your current world with images.

So, imagine you're in your living room wearing augmented reality glasses. You'll see your living room and a virtual cat alongside your daily living.

Virtual reality is when you enter a brand-new world as a whole. Different characters, rule sets and that kind of stuff.

If we are living in a virtual reality, that means the outside world is simply conditioned to our senses. Our senses can perceive time, space & causality conditions. But our senses are vastly different from a dog, butterfly or mosquito.

Which one is real?

As humans, we choose our reality to be the standard reality. And that's all good with me.

As awareness rises, the question: *is there more?*
Are we just bodies?

I don't think that's the case.

We've done a great job in studying the objective world in terms of science. But subjective science is only popular in certain parts of the world, not mainstream yet.

I believe mankind was given the power to create technology to learn more about life.

Not only to learn more about life, but to learn more about themself.

I had to work a lot with computers in my career. This made me notice something.
'What?'
Computers are little humans.

The 4 processes of a computer are:
1. Input
2. Process
3. Store
4. Output

Those are the processes of humans as well.

Input data from the external world.
Process the data via the conscious mind.
Store the data in the memory & subconscious mind.
Output data via language & actions.

Humans use a computer to enter a digital reality. Even though a lot of the stuff on the computer (or phone) screen look like discrete elements...It's all the same.

Same electronic pixels with different colors. But to the perception, it looks "different."

Humans use the computer to enter a digital reality. A reality humans wouldn't be able to enter without the use of a computer.

'Then why do humans exist?'
I don't know. But I do believe we are meant to do something

of value. Something of purpose.

Do we live in a virtual reality?

I'm not sure. But beliefs which I used to think were idiotic make full sense to someone else. Before judging, pause.

We may accumulate knowledge at a later portion of life which allows us to think differently.

Till then, just maintain curiosity and ask questions before ruling things off.

How Teaching Reduces Anxiety

Teaching helps with 2 causes of anxiety.

1. Unused knowledge.
2. Over consumer.

1. Unused Knowledge

Have you ever had that moment when you were reading, watching videos, listening to podcasts without an end goal in mind?

Just mindless consuming.

Well in a situation like that, you are absorbing **a lot** of energy. Unused energy turns into anxiety.

When you teach someone, you are actively turning that knowledge into value. You release the excess energy & help someone along the way. You'll automatically feel a sense of calm. Anxiety will melt.

2. Over consumer

Teaching is a great way to give back & graduate into production mode.

Everyone is a consumer for a certain point in their life. Heck, I'll go as far to say that we never stop being a consumer.

However, what we predominantly do will dictate our

emotional resilience.

When you only are a consumer, you will sense a lack of work ethic on your end.

You'll release dopamine in your mindless consumption which gives you the illusion that you are working, while in reality you got 0 results to show.

Picture the typical armchair quarterback.

When you consume & produce in harmony, now you make it an effort to CREATE value rather than just absorb it. Teaching is an excellent way to be a producer.

A lot of content nowadays is some form of teaching. Mix that with some entertainment & you become unique.

Once again, anxiety will melt.

Ultimately, your goal is to consume to produce & teach. Don't just consume without an end goal in mind. That's like driving without a location in mind.

Teaching rewires your mindset in many ways.

If you are investing your energy into a certain skill set, then make it a priority to teach once you start building competency in your field.

I write this book not only because it's a way to give back...But also, because it helps me out in the process.

A teacher is a weapon in the communications world.

Learn the ways of a teacher & spark a chain of knowledge.

The only way to learn the ways of a teacher is by becoming one for yourself.

The Power of Allies

I love it when I see someone enjoy what they do.
They don't just do it for the paycheck, but they are also very good at it.

The older I get, the more I would prefer quality rather than cheap.

There was this Chinese restaurant that was right by my house. The food was cheap.

However, there was a catch.
'What?'
The quality was awful.

The rice was stale.
Service was awful.
They skimped on the soy sauce.

Eh, you know what? Time to take the business elsewhere.

2 weeks later, I found another Chinese place that was farther, but I heard it was good. Decided to check it out.

This place was more expensive, but the food was 10x better.

This place officially got a new customer.

Whenever I needed Chinese food, I would go to them, despite it being further and more expensive.

Plus, the hostess, Min, who worked there was cool. Her and I built a bond. She knew my name & my order preferences.

One day, I went there & I noticed Min wasn't there. It was a boy in his 20s working. The kid was very rude.

He messed up my order the first time.

When I finally got the order, I asked for hot oil.
He said, 'that will be 50 cents.'

That's strange. Min normally gives it for free. How come he is charging?

Obviously 50 cents isn't too much, so I paid and left.

The next time I went, Min was working again. She gave me the usual and gave the hot oil for free.

That's when I asked, *does the hot oil cost 50 cents?*

She smiled & said, 'yes.'

I asked her how come she normally gives it to me for free?

She said 'it's because you always support us. We want your business.'

Boom!

Just like that, I knew Min was not just a hostess. She had high social intelligence.

The social intelligence played a big role in her business as well. Simply by making a 50-cent investment in ONE customer, she got a routine customer. Plus, that routine customer sent her plenty of business too.

I took my out-of-town friends there & went there with my former coworkers. Plenty of them became go to customers as well.

Min thought big picture. Whether she was aware of it or not.

The 50-cent hot oil may seem small. But it is the principle behind it. The principle behind it allowed her to form an ally.

An ally is defined as the state of formally cooperating with one another.

Min & I were allies.

'You mean you & your restaurant hostess were allies? I thought that was only for very important relationships??' *Important is subjective.*

Anything that has a potential for a relationship has the potential to turn into an ally.

In school, we are taught 1+1 = 2.

But in the real world:
1 +1 can be greater than 2. **That's synergy.**
1 + 1 can be less than 2. **That's dysergy.**

Synergy is an empowering relationship where both people leave the interaction feeling better.

I got my hot oil for free & good food. Min got my business and other people's business as well.
Win-win.

The first Chinese shop right by my house was dysergy.

The Chinese shop got my money. I got stale ass fried rice.
Win-lose.

An ally doesn't need a lot of contracts and all of that.
Sometimes, it happens out of the blue moon.

I had no clue that Min had opted to be my ally, until I found
out that the hot oil she was giving me for free, actually costs
money. No contracts, handshakes, or anything.

Just an invisible bond that connected us 2.

The social world is full of invisible bonds. And this world is
looking for people who want to exchange hot oil for your
business.

How to Become Well Read

During the 5th grade, I knew 2 kids.
Frederick & Doug.

Frederick was this tall, skinny, Haitian kid.
Doug was this fat, pudgy, Puerto Rican kid.

All of us were in the same class. But Frederick & Doug never talked to each other.

One day, there was a girl named Bianca who decided to stir up some drama.

For some reason, she went to Frederick & said Doug had been making fun of him to the other kids in class.

Furious... Frederick went to confront Doug.

Once he did, Doug had no clue what Frederick was talking about.

At that point, one of the funniest things happened.

Frederick said to Doug:
'Boi, you better stop talking about me & go back to digging for that golden CHEEESEE!!'

He said it an extremely animated way.

I had no clue what that meant, but the whole class erupted in laughter. The kid next to me said that Frederick was implying that Doug scratches his butt.

For the next few weeks, Frederick would always bring up that joke to insult Doug, and Doug just took it.

You could tell that he wanted to insult Frederick back, but Doug had no clue what to say.

One day, our 5th grade teacher had the class read out loud from our history book.

One. Person. At. A. Time.

By the time it came to Frederick, he looked *nervous.*

Frederick forcefully tried to read, but the whole process was awkward.
Was he that nervous?

Class bell rang.
Doug smelled blood.

Doug had a huge gut instinct that Frederick couldn't read.

Yea right!
How can you possibly be in the 5th grade & can't read?
That's impossible!

No... Doug may have been onto something.

One day, Frederick insulted Doug in lunch. That's when Doug pulled out a Lord of the Rings book and said:

'I'll give you 20$ if you can read a page from the book & tell me what you just read.'

Frederick looked terrified.

All the other kids looked on. This was EASY money. Only a chump would say no to that.

However, Frederick made some excuse.
Doug & everyone in the cafeteria began laughing hysterically.
'Haha Frederick can't read!!!' yelled Doug enthusiastically.

How the hell are you in the 5th grade and can't read? How did you make it this far?

I thought the issue would have gotten fixed by kindergarten or 1st grade, max.

Nope.
Frederick really couldn't comprehend sentences.

Nowadays, I think about that story with more compassion. There are a lot of people who cannot read.

I saw this 'What Would You Do' episode a while back where the episode was based on a person trying to order on a menu, but didn't know how to read. Others were making fun of him. This is an issue for a segment of the population.

If you are reading this, then you don't have that problem. But a problem that you may have is:
Are you actually reading?

Imagine your life if you couldn't read.

It almost seems like you are missing an arm and a leg.

The key to becoming a good reader is to not just view reading
in terms of completing books.
Instead, viewing it as a lifestyle.

I had an email reader who jokingly said:
'I haven't read a book in a decade. But I always read your
emails! Does that count? Haha.'

Actually, it does.

Reading anything primes the mind to treat reading like a
lifestyle rather than a standalone act. From reading emails, to
tweets, to texts, to nutrition labels, to advertisements etc.

Almost anything worth a damn has words on them. Affirm to
yourself that you ARE reading.

When you affirm to yourself that you are reading, that's
when you get rid of the negative stigma like:
'Books are just for smart people!'

And instead, you'll think:
*'Homie, I read all the time. Why would this book intimidate
me? Give me that!'*

That's a paradigm shift.

It's a game of starting off small.
Find anything that you can get your mind to read.

ACKNOWELDGE that you're engaging in the act of reading,
and naturally build up from there.

I have no clue what Frederick is up to nowadays. But hopefully, he finally learned the skill that has changed many lives.

There is a power to the word.
As famous texts have said:
And the word became flesh.

Why I Like General Goals

In the world of improvement, specific goals get a lot of love. On the flip side, general goals get little to no love.

You can even argue that general goals get hate.

'You didn't get specific? This guy clearly doesn't know what he wants!'

You can also make the argument that someone who gets too specific creates blinders.

They may know what they want at one stage of their life, sure. But people are living information systems.

You ever had that one moment where your mindset regarding a certain issue flipped completely?
'Yes, a *few* times.'

That's not to say you were wishy washy or a bad person. It's to say that new information can lead to new interpretations.

Likewise, with people, new information comes down to new experiences. A goal that we made at age 20 may be night and day different than a goal we make at age 30.

This is why I like the general mindset for long term goals.
'What do you want to be in the future?'
I have a rough idea, but I do not know everything, man.

This is also why I'm not a big fan of announcing goals to

everyone.

It's because a GRAND goal is bought into fruition through a process of iteration. It's not a random light bulb moment that generates out of nowhere.

So I'm a big fan of general goals in terms of a **long term vision.**

What else?

I'm also a big fan of generalities when you **lack experience.**

For a person who is looking to write their first blog, just start.

Rather than setting the goal:
'I need to learn SEO, meta descriptions, keyword research, hosting blah blah blah.'

Just say:
'I have a desire to improve writing.'

This general goal will completely bypass the logical mind. The logical mind loves little details. But the emotional mind heard you loud and clear.

Whenever we stick with a goal long term & do it with consistency, there's always an emotional charge that sparked off the entire process.

Once this guy starts writing the blog posts, now they can gradually add in all those specifics along the way.

So long term goal & activities which you lack experience in

are good times to activate generalities.
Try it out.

With self-improvement, it comes down to finding the right
pattern for a specific personality type.

*What falls flat with one person may be the missing puzzle
piece for another person.*

Even though general goals don't get love...
General goals can activate emotions.

When the emotions are activated, that's when boldness &
creativity can be unleashed in any given field. Something that
being overly specific does not always guarantee.

Importance of Resting

Our culture is very polarized nowadays. There are predominantly 2 groups of people:

One group can't spell rest.
One group can't do anything but rest.

The first group over works.
The second group just sits on their ass.

I want to talk about the first group.
I want to talk about the importance of resting.

When I was working as an engineer, I remember my manager would teach me how to create down times for the systems.

The down time is a period where the system is off, so it can gain its momentum back.

Why would a system need to be off? I thought.

So, curiosity got the best of me & I asked my manager.

'The system needs a downtime so it can produce more effectively' my manager said.
I continued to listen.

'If you overwork the system, then it will corrode faster. Something can't always be at 110%, Armani.'

That got me thinking.

If a machine can't be ON all the time, then I doubt a human can be, right? Well, I had to learn this lesson the hard way.

There was a day when I got very sick out of nowhere. Had a strong fever & was feeling out of it.

However, I had a busy schedule ahead of me. Had to do a few podcast interviews, content creation, networking, working with clients etc.

Fuck being sick, I'm going to take care of business.

Rather than resting, I doubled down on the work.

Results?
Felt 10x worse.

Felt like I was operating with a massive hangover after getting hit by a truck.

My managers words rang once again:

'Something can't always be at 110% Armani.'

Alright body, you win.
So, I rested.

I spent 2 days doing my super high ROI tasks then fell back. Less work.

A few hours of rest sessions in, I automatically noticed something.

The lingering pains of the fever began to melt away.

Clarity rose once again.

I felt reborn.

I felt 10x better & more ready to tackle the day's challenges.

Situations like this make me wonder...

If I felt that much more mentally alert after resting from my sickness, then what if I scheduled in time for resting like I schedule in time for work?

That's exactly what I will be doing from here on out. That's exactly what you should be doing as well.

Have a time limit when you are doing ZERO work.

Full focus on not focusing. Counterintuitive, I know. But assign your machine some downtime.

I mentioned earlier that there are 2 groups.
One that can't rest.
One that can't do anything but rest.

I urge you to fall in the middle. Ditch hustle culture & ditch Netflix culture. Learn the art of doing both.

When you hustle, hustle.
When you chill, chill.

Simple in theory. But when you're a hard worker or super lazy, hard as hell to execute.

3 steps:

1. Identify a time every day when you will rest. Non-negotiable.

2. Have a rough idea of what you will do in that time.

3. No working, just relaxing.

Turn strategic rests into a habit. Guarantee you'll notice a spike in your production.

Fire In the Belly

I've always been curious about musicians for some reason.

Been following rock, hip hop, battle rap & Bollywood music growing up. I have been curious about them because they had to design a lane for themselves.

Music is a creative field, therefore, there is a level of ambiguity that is involved.

There are producers, beat makers & record labels who want structure, don't get me wrong. But ultimately, it is up to the artist to see how far they will take their career.

Growing up, I've seen many artists come and go. They were powerhouses in their prime.

Nowadays? I may not even recognize them if I was walking past them in Walmart.

I'll tell you what changed.
It was the fire in their belly.

The fire in the belly is a level of determination that you operate with.

When you are an up-and-coming artist, you have this level of hunger to you. You want to prove yourself & show that you are a boss.

But when you are given a multi-million-dollar record deal, endorsements & whatever you ask for, the fire *dims*.

Sad.

It's sad because the music industry is a pure 'what have you done for me lately' industry.

To have a long career, you need to have produced so many hits that people have lost count.

Like Michael Jackson, Madonna, Jay Z etc.
2-3 hits ain't gonna cut it homie!

I remember back in the days, 50 Cent ran the world. The year was 2003.

He came out with a banger known as 'In Da Club.' We heard it left and right in my school bus.

That summer, I went to Bangladesh, and I even heard my cousins blasting the song!! 50 was a global phenom.

Recently, I was at the mall & I heard someone in line say:
'Yo! Did you know that guy who created the show Power used to rap?'

These kids!!

50 Cent moved on from music, yes. Good for him. On the other hand, many artists will not be remembered by the next generation because they aren't consistent.

They don't operate with the same hunger that they did when they were coming up.

So how do you fight this ill fate??
You fix your mindset about plateaus.

The reason a lot of people lose their fire is because of
plateaus.

I don't care which field you are in. You don't
consistently grow every single day. That's a fantasy world.

In the real world?

You grow.
Then hit a plateau.

Your first plateau, you panic.
You think you broke something...

But nah, it's normal.
Keep going.

When you're that upcoming rapper, the fire in the belly forces
you to push past the plateau.

When you are that rapper with millions, your contentment
has you approaching the plateau with a defeated attitude.

'Why are so *few* great?'
Because if 'few' were 'many', then great would be ordinary.

Not everyone was meant to be great.

Otherwise, every rapper would be a multi-platinum artist.
Every football player would have a Superbowl trophy. Every
basketball player would be inducted into the hall of fame.

Only a *few* will be great.
The *fire* in their belly never dims.

They have off days just like anyone else. But they are masters at having their eyes on the bigger picture.

Which is why they have pig headed persistence towards plateaus. They have been there & done that.

They know plateaus are setting them up for the next growth zone.

You need to be honest with yourself.

Which boat are you in?
Are you like the many, or the few?

No need to be ashamed. But then again, if you chose the right answer, then ashamed is not even in your vocabulary.

Maintain your fire, my friend. Use it as your engine, fuel & steering wheel.

The end of each plateau holds a new opportunity for growth.

While many fall off in the journey, be the person who others have no choice but to remember.

The Sweet Toxicity

Pretty face & a rotten heart.
Pleasing to the eyes & demonic to the soul.

Have you ever met that one person who seemed like an angel on the surface but was always followed by chaos?

This sweet angel was being accused of drama, spreading gossip & being a snake.

Pretty shocking, right?
No way can this person behave like that.

But no, they can.
Don't undermine human nature, my friend.

When I first got into the University of South Florida, one of my friends from high school was joining me.

Her name was Cindy. A 4-foot little girl, always wearing a dress & had an innocent laugh.

Cindy really helped me out in high school. We met in trigonometry class where she struggled. But since I was good in the subject, I helped her out. Other than being good at trigonometry, I was a straight up loser.

I would rarely have friends to sit with at lunch. And luckily, Cindy changed that.

She went out of her way to introduce me to her friends. She was popular.

Cindy was the student body president who knew everyone & threw the most awesome parties.

Because of her, high school wasn't that bad.

By the time we entered college, it was a game of working together.

I introduced my friends to her squad & she introduced her friends to mine.

Soon enough, we ended up having a similar friend circle. We all watched movies together, attended school events together & went out together. It was great forming such a tight knit bond in a new location.

However, that all took a turn one day.

One afternoon, one of my good friends Peter, said his girlfriend dumped him. I asked him why.

He said that Cindy apparently told his girlfriend that he was flirting with other people.

Peter?? No way!

Peter was socially awkward and could barely talk to me without being weird. I doubt he was flirting with other girls. Plus, he was a very loyal person.

Something seemed strange.
This was just the beginning.

A few weeks later, I heard Cindy's name involved in another piece of drama within our friend group.

Again??

This time, I decided to see if all was good on Cindy's end. I gave her a call to see whatsup.

Her opener:
'Oh my God Armani, I HATE drama.'
(Keep this sentence in mind.)

What began off as a close group of friends soon became divided.

Some people were choosing Cindy's side & some people were choosing the accuser's side.

Not going to lie, the accusers sure as hell were piling up.

It got to a point where I was being asked to choose sides as well. How could I possibly do that?

Cindy looked out for me when I was in high school.

She always had my back.
She was a sister to me.
But something was **peculiar**.

Now that I thought about it, stuff like this happened in high school as well. Cindy was always being put in positions where there was drama involved.

Back then, I thought it was because she was one of the popular kids. Popular kids are always involved in something, right?

What was the explanation for college?

Tarnished social bond after tarnished social bond led me to learn a dark side of social dynamics.

Physical appearance does NOT dictate character.

Cindy was the problem.

She had a sweet looking demeanor of a little princess.

But within?
She was rotten to the core.
She loved drama.
Heck, she thrived off it.

Seeing social groups being pulled apart, being the center of attention for gossip, and having people choose sides made her feel alive.

People who often say (not always), 'OMG I hate drama' are often the ones starting it.

You will notice something about this group.
Where they go, drama follows.

I doubt it's everyone else who is the issue.

Pretty sure the Cindy's in the world are the magnet for drama because they are the root cause.

They are UNAWARE that they are the root cause because they have been doing it for so long, that now it is a subconscious act.

Beware.
Sweet toxicity is something many people fall for.

Good looking people are viewed as more trustworthy by the subconscious mind.

Shallow, I know.
Human nature doesn't give a fuck.

It's silly to give away trust like candy.
It's not Halloween.

Trust is always earned. Trust is one of the primal currencies that is nurtured OVERTIME.

Patience is king.

'How does someone earn my trust?'
Through actions.

The words are empty if the actions aren't congruent with the words.

If you see someone is always starting drama with others, then it's just a matter of time till they start drama with you.

Sweet toxicity is in the air...

Take Back a Cheater?

The emotional intelligence world is a very liberating one & a very daunting one at the same time.

Liberating, because you learn to tame your emotions, regulate energy & empathize.

Daunting because now you see how many people are emotionally unintelligent & how many people are get their emotions played.

I realized how blind people were to the emotional world recently when I saw my buddy going through a tough time.

His girlfriend of 7 years cheated on him.

'7 years?? Whoa, that sucks dude!'
I know.

What sucks more was that he didn't have a clue on what to do about it. Let me tell you a story about Sean and Jenny.

Earth Shattering News

It was just like any other day in the city of Tampa.

I was chilling with 5 close friends at a beach house restaurant for my buddy John's birthday.

It was a boy's night out considering John was going to be moving to Boston in a few weeks. We were chilling, laughing & roasting each other.

What seemed unusual was that one of the guys, Sean, was very quiet. He was always the loudest one who would not shut up.

Today, he was church mouse status.

He was disrupting the energy with his mopey face. After a while, one of the guys decided to ask him what was wrong.

At that point, Sean revealed what was bugging him.

He told us that his girlfriend of 7 years had just cheated on him. He said this while holding back tears & with a shaky voice.

The entire squad was stunned!!!
Jenny cheated on Sean??
Huh???
He **had** to be joking.

'Was he joking??'
No, he was dead serious.

This was stunning news considering Sean & Jenny had been dating for as long as I could remember.

Still recall the exact day they met in class. The entire group genuinely thought they were going to get married.

'Wow, that's some shocking news.'
Wait, that's just the beginning.

Apparently, Sean had forgiven Jenny because she was drunk. This part was surprising to the rest of the squad. We spent the remainder of the dinner convincing him to end it.

Drunk or not, cheating is cheating.

Sean wouldn't have it. He loved Jenny & in his world, this whole thing was a big mistake. Jenny was simply the sweet angel who was taken advantage of when she was drunk.

Nothing more.

A few weeks later

Within a few weeks, Sean began to bring Jenny around again to our events.

You could tell the chemistry between them had been disrupted. Poor eye contact, less joking & a sense of unease.

It got extremely awkward when Jenny made a lighthearted joke regarding Sean's pants.
And he SNAPPED.

He started calling her every name in the book from: Hoe, Slut, Bitch Cunt... you name it.

The vibe had gotten so awkward that we had to pull those 2 apart. Damn, that was so intense that it would be hard to bounce back.

Who knows, love has a funny way of shocking us.

Present Day Moment

'So, what ended up happening?'
Jenny ended up dumping Sean & leaving him for the guy that

she cheated on him with.

'Wait, what??? Where's the happy ending?'
There is none.

This is a look into the dark side of emotional intelligence.

The dark side regarding how alcohol is **really** the truth serum.

If you want to be exposed to the truth, proceed on.

The truth about Alcohol

Wrong: Alcohol makes you do things that you never wanted to do.

Right: Alcohol makes it easier to do things that you always wanted to do.

Keep reading this until you internalize it.

The reason that this happens is because alcohol disengages the logical mind & allows a person to unleash their feelings.

So, the people who cheat, more often than not, had the feelings about doing so for a long time. Their critical mind was just preventing them from doing so when they were sober.

'Wait! So, taking back a person who cheated when they were drunk isn't wise?'
Absolutely not.

If they were black out drunk, I could listen to your argument.

Still...

Do you want someone who puts themselves in that predicament? That's not long-term material.

Life Formula:

Remember this homie.

Your true self comes out when you are:

- o *Angry*
- o *Under pressure*
- o *Given authority*
- o *Given anonymity*
- o *Drunk*

Just like Sean, you don't want to waste your time on trash. And to be honest, you should be a little thankful that the other person got your girl to cheat on you. Because they did **you** a favor.

Would you really want to spend life with a closet cheater?
'No.'
Exactly. They took out the trash for you.

Good riddance.

Reality of Best Friends

People come & go, but the person across the mirror stays the same.

People will always have their main goals, dreams, desires in mind. That's what most of their thought patterns center around.

Which is why people come & go.

Picture your squad from elementary school. Many of you haven't kept in touch with them. And many of you can't even name them without taking time to think about it.

A lot of people who are around you now will not be here within the next year to decade. They will be focusing on their goals, dreams & desires. At times, those goals will not align with yours.

Last year, I was able to get back in touch with a *few* friends who I lost touch with. One of them was my best friend in undergrad.

He hit me up out of the blue moon & told me he was getting married and wanted me to be a groomsman.
I agreed.

Mind you, we randomly stopped talking for 2-3 years. Nothing personal or malicious.

Sort of just gradually began doing our own thing. The gradual increments built up.

But the day we met up for lunch, we picked up right where we left off.

O awkwardness.
Felt as though we didn't skip a beat.

When evaluating great friends, zoom out.

Zooming out will allow you to see how often you guys kept in touch, drifted, and reignited the social bond.

Zooming out will also allow you to see how many chapters of your life this particular friend was involved in.

In the perfect world, we can keep in touch every day. With many of our best friends, we do.

However, a human life is unpredictable.

Different people hit different stages at different times.

That may put a certain distance in the friendship.

When you just stay zoomed in, then you don't see the bigger picture... you may let a blip change the narrative of a potentially good friendship.

When I work, I work. My great friends know when I am in grind mode, they may not consistently hear from me. The great friends accept this. They don't pout & give me the cold shoulder.

Learning about psychology & human nature requires us to realize our mode of thinking isn't necessarily the same mode of thinking for someone else.

And that's fine.

The reality about best friends is that although they may not ALWAYS keep in touch...

The universe always finds a way to reunite them.

If shit goes down & you hit them up for an emergency... They will be the first to help you in any way they can. Look out for these signs.

People come and go, but some will always find a way back...

Autodidact

Transitioning from high school to college is a night and day experience.

In high school, there is less freedom. The student has to show up to class, otherwise, they fail.

But in college, for a lot of classes, showing up is a *choice*. The professor doesn't care if the student attends or not.

What the professor does care about is whether or not the student passes the exams and does the homework.

I had this college professor named Professor Seminole.
A guy in his 70s, full of energy & smart.

He was mainly full of energy when he would stop teaching. During class lectures, he was a boring guy who would read off the PowerPoint slides verbatim.

After class, he was completely different. Super chill.

One day during lecture, he let us know that
he **hated** teaching. He said:
'You kids know that I'm only teaching because they are making me, right? I actually got hired to be a researcher in this school.'

This was a bold statement for a professor to make so openly. He seemed proud.

It's not like university was *free*. There was college tuition,
book costs, room and board involved.

Then again...
The students would joke that college is the place where you
pay to teach yourself.

I learned that day how outdated the school system was. It
was a dinosaur.

Not to say that college was a waste of time. I went onto get
my masters after my bachelors.
So, I understand the importance of formal education.

However, in the age of the internet:
It's the autodidact who wins.

An autodidact is a self-taught person.
- o   A person who needs an internet connection & hustle
    to get started.

These are the only 2 variables to be honest.
Everything else is added on after. From mastermind groups,
club events, buying books etc.

If you are clueless in the age of the internet regarding a field
that you are curious about, then it was a choice. Make no
mistake about that.

For the autodidact, one of the most powerful skills
is **interleaving learning.** This is when subjects are cross
combined to understand patterns.

Multitasking is often reprimanded. It's vilified. But I believe multitasking *incorrectly* should be vilified.

In reality, multitasking can help unlock insane levels of creativity. That's because multitasking showcases the parallel processing of the brain.

The incorrect way to multitask is to be in the gym & pull out your phone mid workout.

The correct way to multitask is on a macro level.

You can learn a skill set like lifting weights & public speaking at the same time.

When lifting weights, lift.
When public speaking, just focus on speech creation & speech delivery.

The autodidact can multitask within the field of learning.
Why?
Because they have no other choice.

While learning public speaking, I noticed I was forced into the world of psychology, persuasion, emotional intelligence, vocal tonality, body language, storytelling, concentration etc.

This was just a natural progression. Not something that happened overnight.

If you told me I had to learn all those subjects when I was learning public speaking, I would have looked at you sideways.

In the information age, it comes down to who can learn, and who can learn efficiently.

Learning one subject at a time is good. But learning only one subject while neglecting all other subjects is intellectual suicide.

Since starting ArmaniTalks, one thing I noticed is that I got pulled back into history as well.
I always loved history in high school because the classes were easy, but never thought it would be applicable in the real world.

That was incorrect.
History repeats itself in different contexts.

What's going on with information technology is what occurred when the printing press was first being engineered.

Meaning, that information is now available to a larger scale.
-For the printing press, it was in the context of national distribution.
-For the information age, it is in the context of global distribution.

Interleaving learning is the engine of the autodidact's spirit. It's when you're self-motivated & don't need someone else to discipline you.

You discipline yourself.

The tools are there. Unfortunately, the college professors I had are in abundance. They are just researchers who are forced to teach.

The ones who do want to teach aren't always the best teachers. And the ones who are the best teachers may not be teaching you the subjects that you need to know in context to your life.

That's where the autodidact in each one of us needs to step up.

There is no blueprint.

Just the desire & the awareness to follow your curiosity.

Symbols to Build Creativity

Creativity is the art of structuring the internal world. It's a game of turning the universe into a cosmos.

The cosmos is the universe with order.

One mistake regarding creativity is thinking that it is completely random. That mindset creates a lopsided philosophy.

Rather, there are 2 modes of the mind.
Synthesis.
Reductionist.

Synthesis portion is for idea creation. It's also known as 'Divergent' thinking. Reductionist portion is for idea refining. This is known as 'Convergent' thinking.

Creativity is perceived as random when the context of convergent thinking & divergent thinking is confused for one another.

A lack of creativity is a sign that the mind has been overly conditioned with the intellect faculty.

This is the true/false area of the mind. A reductionist approach to life. Breaking things down to its smallest parts.

This allows the mind to make logical connections with ease.

The only problem is that relying on this mode of thinking TOO much leads to a stiff mind.

Synthesis thinking extends past logical thinking alone. It is more about acceptance. It's hard to explain with words.

It must be experienced.

When delving into the world of experience, it is meant to be personal towards us. That's why the intellect needs to be trained to become quiet under will.

If creativity is about structuring the internal world, then we need to know what the internal looks like.

In a case like this, staring at a picture of the universe serves a practical purpose.

Reductionist modes of thinking is great for planet earth. Intellect can be leveraged when we are on earth.

But when we expand past the earth alone, we are STRECHED out of the intellect alone.
Intellect starts to get blurry as we force ourselves out of earth stratosphere.

With the intellect turned DOWN, that is when it becomes easier to understand what synthesis thinking is like. It follows a completely different ruleset.

If you are a logical fellow entering the creative world, take your time easing yourself into the new paradigm. Images and symbols speak to the subconscious mind.

It feels strange when you have an overly intellectual mind &
you're looking at symbols.
Feels like you are wasting time. Where are the numbers,
digits & facts?

Different rulesets.
Symbols mean a lot to us on a deeper level.

You'll also notice smart people often extend into fiction books
when they are gaining knowledge.
Because they can perceive their hard-earned lessons through
the paradigm of symbols.

*A good fiction book is meant to help you evolve past word
only thinking to picture thinking.*

**Fire & the universe are the 2 best symbols to turn the
intellect down & unlock elevated levels of creativity.**

When you have writer's block or any creativity block, these
are the 2 symbols to leverage.

Creativity requires the individual to adopt an experiential
mode of thinking rather than only dissecting.

When you unlock your inner creativity, it's easier to see the
similarities between an artist and an engineer.

What an engineer does in the external world is virtually what
the artist does in the internal world.

They do the same things of creation, connection &
refining, just on 2 different planes.

Afterward

Thank you for making it to the end of this book. Hopefully, you got some takeaways which allow you to view life in a different way.

The life of growth mode is very much different than a fixed mindset. What the fixed mindset considers to be work, the growth mindset does for pleasure.

An example is learning to apply.
The application process alone seems like work.

But when you know *why* you are doing what you are doing, the whole game changes.

In the modern culture, it's easy to make fun of knowledge. Mainly because it's seen as a form of procrastination in some circles.

'Quit reading so much and finally do!'
That's what certain self-improvement circles parrot away.

Are these people wrong?
Sort of.

Sure, if a person only reads all day, that's probably not the best use of their time. The knowledge should be applied at one point or another.

However, if a person gains that knowledge and works in tandem with the application process, now the whole game changes.

We need to defy gravity.

Too many of us are thinking in terms of physical states only, and that is a problem.

The physical world is a beautiful playing field that allows us to use the world of structures and potentially become creators. However, the physical world with neglect to the mental world creates issues.

We were meant to explore the universe, stars, and galaxies. Not in a rocket ship. But with our imagination leading the way.

Hopefully, after reading this book, you see life in a new way in a certain field. Even if it only took 1 story to change your perspective.

If you enjoyed my writing style, then be sure to check me out on www.armanitalks.com.

In my website, you'll be connected to my YouTube videos, blogs, podcasts, other books, services and much more.

I also run a free daily newsletter where you can sign up at www.armanitalks.com/newlsetter.

In this email list, I discuss topics ranging from public speaking, social skills, emotional intelligence, creativity, storytelling, and level up mindset.

Apply the knowledge you learn, my friend.

Have the stomach to make mistakes.
Learn from those mistakes.
Then refine along the way.

A Limit Breaker fuels their spirit daily so they can fly to the uncharted territories of life.

One galaxy at a time...

ARMANITALKS